Dedicated to the Pioneers
Who Passed Through Angel Island

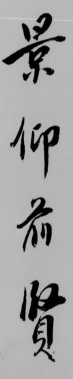

ACKNOWLEDGEMENTS

To Smiley Jann, Tet Yee, Mak Takahashi, Alexander Weiss, George Araki, and The Chinese Historical Society of America, we owe our deepest gratitude for making this collection available to posterity. We are also much indebted to Dr. Kai-yu Hsu, Dr. James Liu, Mr. Yuk Ow, the late Mr. Gilbert Woo, Kay Boyle, and Dr. Edmond Yee for contributing their time and expertise in proofreading our translations, to David Shew and Bing-Zi Press for the Chinese typesetting, to Mr. Goon K. Lum and Mr. Kew Yuen Ja for the calligraphy, and to Laura J. Lai, Martin Jue, Sandra Lee, Wei-chi Poon, Dr. Thomas Wu, James P. Lee, Martin H. Eber, Kelsey Street Press, the Chinese Culture Foundation of San Francisco, Janice Mirikitani and Ed Nathan of The Zellerbach Family Fund, and San Francisco Study Center for their assistance and support.

ISLAND
Poetry and History of Chinese Immigrants
on Angel Island
1910-1940

BY

HIM MARK LAI, GENNY LIM, JUDY YUNG

Published by
HOC DOI
(History of Chinese Detained on Island)

A project of the Chinese Culture Foundation of San Francisco

DESIGN:
San Francisco Study Center, Harry Driggs

LAYOUT & PRODUCTION:
Andrea Ja

PHOTO CONSULTANT:
Chris Huie,
Kearny Street Workshop

DISTRIBUTED BY:
San Francisco Study Center
P.O. Box 5646
San Francisco, CA 94101

LITHOGRAPHY:
Robert Owen Litho

©1980, HOC DOI Project

Library of Congress #79-67111
ISBN   0-936434-00-7   soft
             0-936434-01-5   hard

This book was made possible by funds from The Zellerbach Family Fund and the Wallace A. Gerbode Foundation.

CONTENTS

INTRODUCTION. 8

TRANSLATORS' NOTE 30

THE VOYAGE
POEMS 1-11 34
ORAL HISTORIES. 44

THE DETAINMENT
POEMS 12-33 52
ORAL HISTORIES. 72

THE WEAK SHALL CONQUER
POEMS 34-46 84
ORAL HISTORIES. 96

ABOUT WESTERNERS
POEMS 47-56 100
ORAL HISTORIES. 108

DEPORTEES, TRANSIENTS
POEMS 57-69 122
ORAL HISTORIES. 136

IMPRISONMENT IN THE WOODEN BUILDING. 138

APPENDIX: POEMS 1-66 150

SOURCES OF POEMS. 171

SOURCES OF PHOTOGRAPHS 171

ENGLISH BIBLIOGRAPHY. 172

CHINESE BIBLIOGRAPHY. 173

INTRODUCTION

Angel Island, now an idyllic state park out in San Francisco Bay not far from Alcatraz, was the point of entry for the majority of the approximately 175,000 Chinese immigrants who came to America between 1910 and 1940. Modeled after New York's Ellis Island, the site was used as the immigration detention headquarters for Chinese a-waiting jurisdiction on the outcomes of medical examinations and immigration papers. It was also the holding ground for deportees awaiting transportation back to the motherland. The ordeal of immigration and detention left an indelible mark in the minds of many Chinese, a number of whom wrote poetry on the barrack walls, recording the impressions of their voyage to America, their longing for families back home, and their outrage and humiliation at the treatment America accorded them.

When the center's doors shut in 1940, one of the most bitter chapters in the history of Chinese immigration to America came to a close. The poems expressing the thoughts of the Chinese immigrants were locked behind those doors and soon forgotten. Those poems have been resurrected and preserved in this book. It was by accident that they have survived. The three of us, offspring of Angel Island inmates, plunged into the project of translation and historical documentation as a personal hobby which later evolved into this book. The task to preserve the words and history of these Chinese immigrants was made more urgent by the fact that most of these old-timers are now elderly and many already have died.

In an effort to discover and document life at the Angel Island Immigration Station, 39 persons—eight women and 31 men,—have been interviewed. Of them, 32 had been detainees at the station. The remainder had visited or worked there. As a whole, the former detainees hesitated to reveal an unpleasant past they preferred left forgotten. It was only after a promise of anonymity that they agreed to be interviewed for this book. Piecing together their recorded testimonies, we can glimpse into their lives on the island, and better understand their motivations for journeying to *Gam Saan,* the Golden Mountain, and their impressions of that immigration experience.

Remarkably enough, detailed experiences occurring 40 to 70 years past ring with a surprising accuracy and clarity. In some cases, as must be expected, generalized descriptions of people and events admittedly are blurred or dulled by the lapse in time. We must bear in mind also the monolingual perspective of the immigrant at the time of detainment. Because of the communication block between the detainees and the immigration authorities, occasional actions and events were not surprisingly misconstrued. But overall, the oral history of the detainees gives a fairly consistent and accurate picture of the immigrants' daily life on Angel Island.

The Chinese detention barrack on Angel Island, a two-story wood building located on a hill overlooking San Francisco Bay, stood abandoned for more than two decades until it was finally marked by the government for destruction. In 1970, park ranger Alexander Weiss noticed characters inscribed on

A door into imprisonment.

the walls inside and concluded they were writings left by Chinese immigrants once detained there for questioning. Weiss informed his superiors but they did not share his enthusiasm or belief in the significance of the calligraphy on the walls. Weiss contacted Dr. George Araki of San Francisco State University, who along with San Francisco photographer Mak Takahashi went out to the island and photographed practically every inch of the barrack walls that bore writing, most of which was poetry. Their discovery soon sparked enough local Asian American community interest to lobby for its preservation, and in 1976 the Legislature appropriated $250,000 for the preservation of the building.

The Chinese began emigrating to America in large numbers during the California Gold Rush. Political chaos and economic hardships at home forced them to venture overseas to seek a better livelihood. From the beginning, they were mistreated. Discrimination was the norm. Forced from the rich gold fields to lean claims disdained by white miners, the Chinese worked hard to eke out a living. In 1852, a Foreign Miner's Tax, which accounted for more than half of the tax revenue collected in California between 1850 and 1870, was imposed on Chinese miners.

Although the Chinese were not welcomed, their contributions to America were important. The Chinese found work in many fields. They were instrumental in building the transcontinental railroads, reclaiming swamplands in California's Sacramento-San Joaquin River delta area, developing the shrimp and abalone fisheries, the opulent Napa-Sonoma vineyards, new strains of fruit, and providing needed labor for California's growing agriculture and light industries. Nonethe-

less, the Chinese continued to be the target of racist laws.

San Francisco passed ordinances such as the Cubic Air Ordinance in 1870, forbidding Chinese to rent rooms with fewer than 500 cubic feet of air per person (for economic reasons most Chinese shared small tenement rooms); the Sidewalk Ordinance in 1870, prohibiting Chinese from using poles to carry laundry loads on the sidewalk; and the Queue Ordinance in 1873, requiring Chinese prisoners to cut their hair short, a disgrace to Chinese nationals in those days. On occasion, when hatred flared, blood-thirsty mobs would storm the Chinese settlements, looting, lynching, burning, and driving the Chinese out. So cruelly did America treat them that it caused humorist Mark Twain to wince and write wryly of the Chinese, "They are a harmless race when white men either let them alone or treat them no worse than dogs."

The Chinese Exclusion Act of 1882 was the inevitable culmination of a series of oppressive anti-Chinese laws and violent physical assaults upon the Chinese. Demagogic politicians and opportunistic labor leaders led the battle for its passage, using the Chinese as a scapegoat for high unemployment during the post-Civil War recession. They stirred the working class into believing that the Chinese were undesirable aliens who deprived whites of jobs. The visible presence of the Chinese and their willingness to take on low-paying menial jobs disdained by whites made them an easy object of scorn.

10

Male detainees on hospital steps.

The Exclusion Act of 1882 heralded a change in the nation's immigration pattern. Free and unrestricted immigration was replaced by restrictions and racism. For the first time in American history, members of a specific ethnic group were refused entry and admittance to the naturalization process. Only government officials, merchants, students, teachers, visitors, as well as those claiming U.S. citizenship were admitted. The Exclusion Act was revised several more times, closing loopholes and becoming stricter in its provisions, so that by the turn of the century, the restriction process was consciously and actively moving toward total exclusion.

However, during these same years life in China was becoming increasingly difficult as China's economy continued to decline under the pressures exerted by Western imperialism. Many were driven abroad to seek better living conditions. Despite the unfriendly environment in the United States, the Chinese were willing to sacrifice lives' savings and risk heavy debts to chance a better life in America. Some traveled to Canada, Mexico, or the Caribbean Islands, where they were smuggled into the United States. Others took advantage of legal loopholes, using credentials of questionable validity.

U.S. immigration officials reacted with harsh measures in order to suppress illegal entries. They frequently swept through Chinese establishments, ensnaring alleged illegal immigrants. Between 1901 and 1910, deportations averaged 560 per year. (It is said that the common sight of khaki-clad immigration officials arresting Chinese gave rise to the Cantonese term, *luk yi,* or "green clothesman," which eventually became the Chinese American colloquial name for "police officer.") At ports of entry, immigration inspectors held all Chinese claims for right of admission suspect until their identities could be verified through cross-examinations. Designed to exclude rather than to admit, routine interrogations of new Chinese arrivals were intensive and detailed.

The Chinese viewed the exclusion laws and regulations as unfair and discriminatory and termed the statutes *keli,* meaning "tyrannical laws." They addressed numerous complaints to the United States government and to Chinese diplomats stationed in this country, objecting to the harsh treatment of the Chinese in general and protesting in particular the suspicious and discourteous attitude immigration officials evidenced toward members of the exempt classes. To protest the immigration procedures, Chinese merchants organized a boycott of American goods which started in Shanghai in 1905 and spread to Canton and other Chinese cities as well as many overseas Chinese communities. Sustained several months, the boycott forced the United States to relax some of its more objectionable regulations. The negative attitude among immigration authorities toward Chinese immigration, however, remained unchanged.

The immigrants' first view of Angel Island barracks.

Until 1910, Chinese ship passengers arriving at San Francisco were detained in a two-story shed at the Pacific Mail Steamship Company wharf (known to the Cantonese Chinese immigrants as *muk uk* or "wooden house") until immigration inspectors could examine them and determine the validity of their claims. As many as 400 to 500 people were crammed into the facility at one time. Chinese community leaders in Chinatown, alarmed at the unsafe and unsanitary conditions of the structure, complained frequently to U.S. officials. Upon investigation, the Immigration Department did indeed find support for the complaints and recommended that funds be appropriated to erect an immigration station on Angel Island to accommodate aliens, chiefly Chinese and other Asians. The subsequent decision to relocate the station to Angel Island was not altogether humanitarian. Officials also felt that the island location would effectively prevent Chinese immigrants from communicating with Chinese on the outside and would isolate immigrants with allegedly "communicable diseases prevalent among aliens from oriental countries." Also, the station, like Alcatraz prison, would be escape-proof.

On January 21, 1910, the Angel Island station officially opened, despite complaints by leaders from San Francisco's

Chinatown that its location was inconvenient for Chinese witnesses. The government quickly discovered that the insular location of the station was unsatisfactory, although they came to the conclusion for different reasons. A few months after the facility opened, acting Commissioner Luther Steward submitted reports to the Commissioner General of Immigration in Washington, D.C., highly critical of the many physical and sanitary drawbacks in the facility's design. In 1920, Immigration Commissioner Edward White declared that the facility's structures were virtual tinder boxes, and he proposed removing the station to the mainland to cut expenses. By 1922, both Assistant Secretary of Labor Edward J. Henning and Commissioner General of Immigration W.W. Husband agreed and Husband declared that the island facilities were filthy and unfit for habitation. But it was not until 1940, when a fire destroyed the administration building, that the government finally abandoned the immigration station. On November 5, the last group of Angel Island detainees, numbering 125 Chinese men and 19 women, was transferred to temporary quarters at 801 Silver Avenue in San Francisco.

After the closing of the immigration station during World War II, Congress, in an attempt to buttress Chinese resistance to Japan on the Chinese mainland and to minimize the effects of the Japanese propaganda attacking American racist policies, repealed the exclusion acts of 1943 and assigned an annual token immigration quota of 105 to the Chinese. Chinese arrivals, however, were still detained to determine the validity of their applications for admission. After being relocated to Sharp Park, California, in the spring of 1942, the detention quarters were moved once again in 1944 into the Appraiser's Building at 630 Sansome Street near San Francisco's waterfront. The detainment of Chinese to determine admission eligibility was finally stopped in the early 1950s when consular officials, responsible for the issuance of visas at the port of embarkation, also assumed the primary responsibility of determining the validity of an applicant's claim by means of submitted documents and interviews.

During the period when the Angel Island Immigration Station was active, immigration officials climbed aboard and inspected the passengers' documents each time a ship arrived in San Francisco. Those with satisfactory papers could go ashore, and the remainder were transferred to a small steamer and ferried to the island immigration station to await hearings on their applications for entry. Although a few whites and other Asians were held on occasion at the detention center, the majority of detainees were Chinese.

As soon as the ferry docked at Angel Island, whites were separated from other races, and Chinese were kept apart from Japanese and other Asians. Men and women, including husbands and wives, were separated and not allowed to see or communicate with each other again until they were admitted into the country.

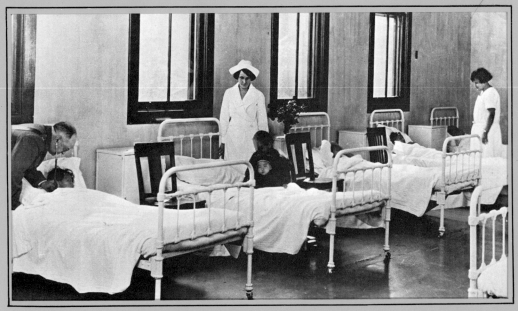
Women's infirmary.

Children under age twelve or so were assigned to the care of their mothers. Most of the Chinese immigrants, however, were males in their teens or early twenties.

Soon after arrival, they were taken to the hospital for medical examinations. Because of poor health conditions in rural China, some immigrants were afflicted with parasitic diseases. The U.S. government classified certain of these ailments as loathsome and dangerously contagious and sought to use them as grounds to deny admission. Arrivals with trachoma were excluded in 1903. In 1910, government officials added to the list uncinariasis (hookworm) and filiariasis and in 1917, clonorchiasis (liver fluke). Because these regulations primarily affected the Chinese, many considered them arbitrary barriers erected to thwart their entry. After considerable protests by Chinatown leaders, some patients were allowed to stay for medical treatment.

Chinese who passed the medical hurdle returned to their dormitories to await hearings on their applications. Men and women lived in separate sparsely furnished communal rooms provided with rows of single bunks arranged in two or three tiers. Privacy was minimal. Men were kept on the second floor of the detention barracks, which was surrounded by a fence to prevent escapes. The women, originally detained in the same building, were moved to the second story of the administration building in the 1920s.

Guards sat outside the dormitories' locked doors, and the Chinese were usually left alone. During the first year of operation, Tye Leung, a Chinese American from Donaldina Cameron's Presbyterian Mission Home in San Francisco, was hired as interpreter and assistant to the matrons, who were technically guards of the women detainees. In 1912, she married a fellow employee, immigration inspector Charles Frederick Schulze, and in the prevailing racist atmosphere of the times, she and her husband were soon forced to resign their positions.

At any one time between 200 and 300 males and 30 to 50 females were detained at Angel Island. Most were new arrivals, but some were returning residents with questionable documents. Also confined were earlier arrivals whose applications had been denied and who were waiting either decisions on their appeals or orders for their departure, Chinese who had been arrested and sentenced to be deported, and transients en route to and from countries neighboring the United States, especially Mexico and Cuba.

To prevent the smuggling of coaching information to detainees prior to interrogation, no inmate could receive outside visitors before his case had been judged. Authorities routinely inspected letters and gift packages to and from detainees for possible coaching messages.

Confined inside the dormitory, the immigrants languished on their bunks, spending their waking hours daydreaming or worrying about their futures. Some passed the time gambling, but stakes were usually inconsequential because the inmates had little pocket money. The literate read Chinese newspapers sent from San Francisco and books brought from home as well as those left behind by others. By the late 1920s or early 1930s, a phonograph and Chinese opera records purchased by the detainees were also available for their amusement. Some women, on the other hand, passed the time sewing or knitting.

Separate small, fenced, outdoor recreation yards afforded the men and women sunlight and fresh air. Once a week they were escorted to a storehouse at the dock where they could select needed items from their baggage. Women and children were sometimes allowed to walk the grounds in a supervised group, a privilege denied the men.

Other than immigration officials, the outsider seen most often by the Chinese immigrants was Deaconess Katharine Maurer (1881-1962), who had been appointed in 1912 by the Women's Home Missionary Society of the Methodist Episcopal Church to do Chinese welfare work at the immigration station. Her work was also supported by funds and gifts from the Daughters of the American Revolution. The deaconess, who became known as the "Angel of Angel Island," helped detainees write letters, taught them English, and performed other small services, primarily for the women and children, to make detention life more bearable.

The San Francisco Chinese YMCA, at Maurer's request, also made regular monthly or biweekly visits to the station. From the 1920s until the station closed, visiting YMCA groups showed movies, taught English, brought newspapers and recreational equipment, and performed small services to help alleviate the tedium and depression of detainment. Clergymen from Chinatown's Protestant missions usually also came on these visits to preach to the inmates. One of the most frequent visitors was Rev. Daniel Wu of the Episcopal Mission. Others were K. Y. Tse of the Presbyterian Mission and B. Y. Leong of the Congregational Mission. However, neither Maurer nor these other visitors could change the basic prison-like conditions created by discriminatory exclusion laws and, despite their persistence, they converted few inmates to Christianity.

The Chinese held at Angel Island understandably resented their long confinements, particularly because they knew that immigrants from other countries were processed and released within negligibly short periods. Disgruntled feelings were fueled by the enforced idleness and unsatisfactory conditions at the station. Unable to change or improve their situation, they frequently petitioned the Chinese Consolidated Benevolent Association, the Chinese Chamber of Commerce, and the Chinese consul general for help. The first petition charging mistreatment was sent only a few days after the station opened in 1910.

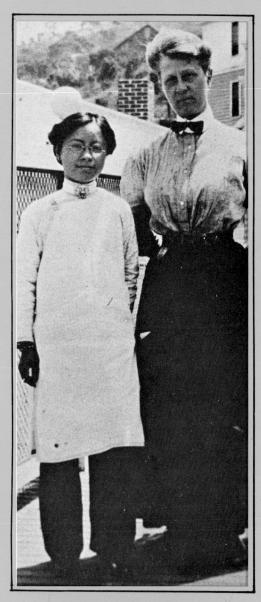

Assistant to the matrons Tye Leung with Deaconess Katharine Maurer.

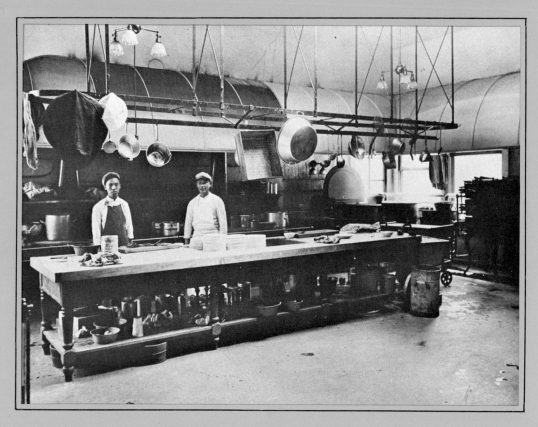

Chinese kitchen cooks commuted from San Francisco.

The detainees' major complaint, especially during the early years, was the quality of food. The concession for providing meals was awarded to private firms based on competitive bids. The quality of the food was debatable. Impatient and angry young immigrants at times staged disturbances in the dining hall located in the administration building, protesting the unpalatable food. These disturbances were rarely reported by the press, but apparently there were enough disturbances to precipitate the posting of a sign in Chinese warning diners not to make trouble nor spill food on the floor. In 1919, a full-fledged riot broke out, and federal troops were called in to restore order. A year later, authorities in Washington, D.C., finally decided to improve the situation and better food was served.

In later years, the food appeared to be nutritionally adequate although hardly comparable to home-cooked meals, as many immigrants remember the meals with distaste. But the generally unfriendly treatment of Chinese at the station, compounded by their anxieties about their futures, undoubtedly contributed to these negative reactions.

In 1922, the male detainees formed an organization called the *Zizhihui* (Self-governing Association), whose purpose was to provide mutual aid and to maintain self-order. Its Anglicized name, ironically, was Angel Island Liberty Association. The concept of forming an organ-ization for collective redress was an old one. Its formation on Angel Island was apparently advocated by politically progressive male detainees. Association officers were usually elected from the people who had been detained the longest, particularly those whose cases were on appeal and, on occasion, respected intellectuals. There was no corresponding organization among the women.

The scope of the association's activities varied from one administration to another. As new immigrants arrived, the association welcomed them and oriented them to life at the dormitory. In this manner, the association was able to provide a social structure that could survive and sustain its transient membership. With meager funds collected from membership dues, the association bought records, books, and recreational equipment for the detainees' amusement. When talent permitted, the association scheduled weekly skits, operas, or musical concerts for evening diversion. At times, classes were organized for children. Occasionally, officers succeeded in curtailing gambling in the dormitory.

Letters to and from detainees often were relayed by the officers of the group. If immigrants had complaints or requests, the association's spokesman, who usually knew some English, negotiated with the authorities. The association's officers also acted as liaisons between the government officials and the inmates.

Some time after the immigrant arrived, he would receive a summons to appear for a hearing on his application for admission. The outcome of the hearing would determine whether he would be admitted to the United States or deported back to China. During the early years of the Angel Island station, this waiting period could stretch into months, which became a source of many complaints. By the mid-1920s, however, the delay averaged two to three weeks.

Regardless of the validity of the Chinese arrival's claim for entry, he or she prepared for an extensive interrogation by memorizing coaching information provided months before the voyage. Facts pertaining to family, home life, and native village were studied in minute detail from coaching books which might run several dozen pages. This was particularly true in cases where the applicant and his witnesses claimed fictitious relationships. Coaching papers were frequently taken aboard ship for review and thrown overboard or destroyed as the ship approached the American harbor.

During the early years, the Chinese complained about the procedure for examination of applicants and witnesses. In 1919, the procedure was changed and a system using boards of special inquiries was instituted, putting Chinese on the same footing with other aliens. A board of special inquiry was made up of two inspectors, one of whom was the chairman who asked most of the questions, and a stenographer. This board was not bound by technical rules of procedure or evidence as applied by federal courts. The board could use any means it deemed fit under the exclusion acts and immigration laws to ascertain the applicant's legitimacy to enter the United States.

Many of the immigrants entered the country as members of the exempt classes, but by far the greater number applied for entry claiming citizenship by birth or by derivation. The majority of Chinese cases involved issues of relationship to natives or actual American birth. Because independent evidence and documents usually did not exist to corroborate or disprove the claims, the scope and method of examination for Chinese cases were different from that applied to immigrants of other nationalities. Evidence was often confined to the testimony offered by the applicant and his witness, and the objective of the board was to determine the validity of this evidence by cross-examination and comparison of testimony on every matter which might reasonably tend to show whether or not the claim was valid. Under these department guidelines, the board of inquiry had great latitude in pursuing its interrogations.

Some inspectors were strict but fair; others delighted in matching wits with the interrogee; still others were thorough and meticulous. The type of question asked often depended on the individual case and the chairman's approach. Over the years, the Chinese persistently complained they were questioned on minute

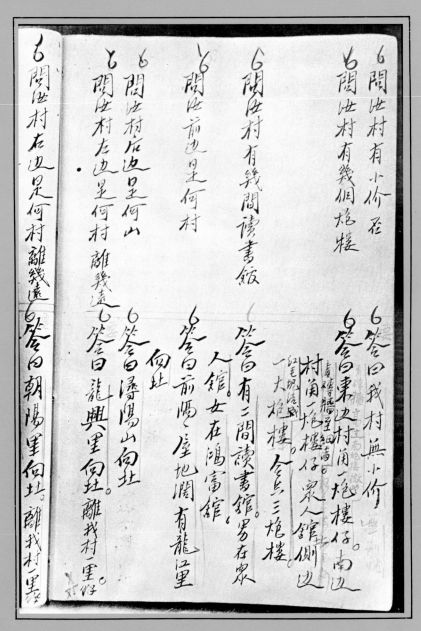

Coaching books were memorized, then destroyed.

details which had no apparent relevance to the objectives of the board. Some queries would have been difficult for anyone to answer: How many times a year did you receive letters from your father? How did your father send you money to travel to the United States? How many steps were there to the front door of your house? Who lived in the third house in the second row of houses in your village? Of what material was the floor in your bedroom? Where was the rice bin located?

Because Chinese immigrants usually did not understand English and the inspectors did not speak fluent Chinese, if any at all, an interpreter was provided at hearing proceedings. To forestall collusion between the applicant and witnesses, a different interpreter was used for each session. At the end of each session, the board chairman usually asked the interpreter to identify the dialect being spoken in order to ascertain whether the applicant and witnesses alleged to be members of the same family were speaking the same dialect.

Sometimes applicants and witnesses were recalled and reinterrogated about questionable points. A typical proceeding usually lasted two or three days. During these interrogations, memories might fail, wrong answers might be given, and unforeseen questions might be asked. Hence, it was often necessary to smuggle coaching information into the detention quarters to eliminate inconsistencies in answers.

The Angel Island Liberty Association served as a link in the communication system between the detainees and the San Francisco community, relaying coaching messages addressed to individual detainees. This system depended upon the cooperation of Chinese employees at the station. The predominantly Chinese kitchen help would visit San Francisco's Chinatown on their off days and pick up coaching messages left by relatives of detainees at specified stores. For a small fee, they would smuggle the messages into the station and pass them at mealtimes to the table closest to the kitchen, where the association's officers dined. The officers had a tacit understanding that if a guard was to detect the existence of a message, they would, if need be, physically prevent its confiscation so that it could not be used as material evidence to jeopardize someone's entry to the country.

If the testimony of the applicant largely corroborated that of the witness, the authorities would land him. On the other hand, if an unfavorable decision was handed down, the applicant would be deported back to China, unless his family counsel appealed to the courts or to higher authorities in Washington, D.C., to reverse the judgment. As a result, some immigrants languished on Angel Island for as long as two years before their cases were finally decided.

Most of the debarred swallowed their disappointment and stolidly awaited their fate. However, some, it was recalled, committed suicide aboard returning ships. There were also suicides in the barracks; but information documenting such occurrences is not readily available. Other discouraged applicants vented their frustrations and anguish by writing or carving Chinese poems on the detention center's walls as they waited for the results of appeals or orders for their deportation.

These poets of the exclusion era were largely Cantonese villagers from the Pearl River Delta region in Guangdong Province in South China. They were immigrants who sought to impart their experiences to countrymen following in their footsteps. Their feelings of anger, frustration, uncertainty, hope and despair, self-pity, homesickness, and loneliness filled the walls of the detention barrack. Many of their poems were written in pencil or ink and eventually covered by coats of paint. Some, however, were first written in brush and then carved into the wood.

Throughout the period the island facilities were used, few Chinese regarded these poems as important. Fortunately, Smiley Jann, detained in 1931, and Tet Yee, detained in 1932, took time to copy most of the poems shown on the walls. Jann copied 92 poems in a manuscript entitled, "Collection of Autumn Grass: Volume Collecting Voices From the Hearts of the Weak" (Qiu Peng Ji—Ji Ruozhe Zhi Xin Sheng Juan"). He later wrote an article for a Shanghai periodical, Renjianshi, recounting his experiences in detention and quoted five poems from his collection. Yee copied 96 poems in all, 78 of which are also in Jann's collection. There are numerous textual differences between the Jann and Yee poems, which may have been due in part to different interpretations of barely legible characters on the walls and to further editing and refining by the compilers.

In 1941, the station was turned over to the U.S. Army. During World War II, the walls were repainted and the barracks were used to hold Japanese prisoners of war, who added their own inscriptions of names, addresses, and slogans. When the Army left the facility, the island became a state park. The structure stood forlorn and neglected, deteriorating under the attacks of natural elements.

Today, more than 135 poems from Angel Island barracks have been recorded. These include the Jann and Yee collection, the Takahashi photographs, poems printed in Three Generations of Chinese, East and West, San Francisco Weekly, Chinese Pacific Weekly, Tien Sheng Weekly, and a collection of Cantonese literature, Yuehai Chunqiu, as well as rubbings made by Kearny Street Workshop members and poems copied by Carson Woo, Allen T. Fong, and a Mr. Chen of New York. Many of these poems are still visible on the walls today. They appear to have been written for the most part either by those detained for a long time or by those awaiting deportation. The majority of the poems are undated and unsigned, probably for fear of retribution from the authorities. Judging from the few that are dated and the fact that two-thirds of the poems in the Jann and Yee collections can still be identified on the walls, a great number of them were written before the 1930s.

The exercise yard.

By that time, the writing of classical poetry was already on the wane in China and few young immigrants coming after 1930 wrote in that style.

The poets borrowed liberally from one another, repeating each other's phrases and allusions. At least two poems (Nos. 15, 33) are imitative of similar works well-known in classical Chinese literature. There are frequent references or allusions to famous literary or heroic figures in Chinese legend and history, especially those who faced adversity. Such literary references may make it difficult for the non-Chinese reader to follow the drift of some poems. For this reason appropriate annotations have been added where necessary.

There are also indications that some poems might have been written by one person and revised by another at some later date. A very obvious example is poem 63. The poem found on the wall today has 10 lines of four characters each. Yet both Jann and Yee apparently saw and copied a poem with five characters per line. (Poem 44 is in Appendix.) However, the sense of each corresponding line, whether written with four or five lines, is the same for the three different versions.

The early twentieth century saw an increasing national consciousness among the Chinese, a spirit which was reflected in the subject matter of the poems. At least half of them voice resentment at being confined and bitterness that their weak motherland cannot intervene on their behalf. There is the recurring defiant wish for China to become powerful enough one day to wreak vengeance on America.

Aside from these basic sentiments, the poems as a whole are not strongly political. Most of the poems bemoan the writer's own situation. A few are farewell verses written by deportees, while others are messages of tribulations by transients to or from Mexico and Cuba.

All of the poems are written in the classical style. Of these, about half are written with four lines per poem and seven characters per line. About a fifth have eight lines per poem and seven characters per line. The remainder consist of verses with six or more than eight lines and five or seven characters per line. There are also a few poems with lines of four characters each, as well as several couplets and one long composition written in the *pianwen* style (a euphuistic style utilizing parallel-constructed couplets with antithetical meanings), published in a San Francisco Chinese newspaper.

The literary quality of the poems varies greatly. The style and language of some works indicate that the poets were well-versed in the linguistic intricacies of poetic expression, while others, at best, can only be characterized as sophomoric attempts.

Most immigrants at that time did not have formal schooling beyond the primary grades. Also for obvious reasons, they were usually not equipped with rhyme books or dictionaries. Created under such conditions, many poems violate rules of rhyme and tone required in Chinese poetry. Incorrect characters and usages are common. (These have been corrected in the printed versions where possible.) Some works have obscure meanings because of the frequent inclusion of Cantonese vernacular expressions as well as Chinese American colloquialisms. Such flaws, if such they are, are not evident in the English translations, because by the very act of translating from the original Chinese into the English language, new literary works have been created which, while keeping the meaning of the original, hide some of the defects.

Regrettably, none of the collected poems were written by women. Women once detained on the island have referred to poems on the walls of the dormitory. Given the fact of the great preponderance of male immigrants and also the fact that during that period most women did not have many opportunities to become educated, it is doubtful whether there were ever many works by female detainees. However, whatever had been written will never really be known. During most

The dining hall.

Meals were noisy, crowded affairs.

The administration building burning in the background.

of the period the station was active, the women's quarters were located in the Center's administration building, which was destroyed by fire in 1940.

Sixty-nine poems were selected on the basis of content and artistry. However, for those interested in reading all the Angel Island poems,—at least those still legible—we have included the remainder in the Appendix.

There may be some argument over the literary merits of the verses, but it is not our purpose to present a case for artistic excellence. These poems stand on their own. Often haunting and poignant in their directness and simplicity of language, they express a vitality of indomitability never before identified with the Chinese Americans. The stereotypic image of a passive, complacent race of lotus-eaters will hardly find substantiation in the following pages.

The poems occupy a unique place in the literary culture of Asian America. These immigrant poets unconsciously introduced a new sensibility, a Chinese American sensibility using China as the source and America as a bridge to spawn a new cultural perspective. Their poetry is a legacy to Chinese Americans who would not be here today were it not for these predecessors' pioneering spirit. Their poetry is also a testimony to the indignity they suffered coming here.

statuses led many Chinese to regard immigration officers as people to avoid and fear. The insensitive attitude of the authorities toward Chinese immigrants only reinforced these sentiments. Moreover, the feeling among Chinese that they were allowed into this country only on the sufferance of the dominant white majority, helped to foster alienation and uninvolvement in the larger society. Dreams of retiring one day to China with small fortunes helped them endure their

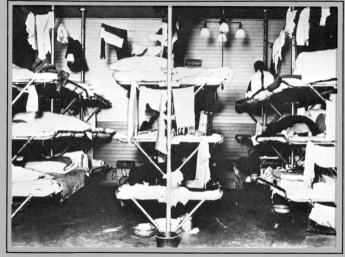

Dormitory

The irony of exclusion was that it did not improve the white workingman's lot. Unemployment remained high and the wage level did not rise after the "cheap" competition had been virtually eliminated. As for the Chinese, their experiences on Angel Island and under the American exclusion laws laid the groundwork for the behavior and attitudes of an entire generation of Chinese Americans. Unpleasant memories as well as shaky legal

treatment as an inferior, undesirable race. But many never realized that dream and instead remained stranded in this country, living out their lives as lonely bachelors, separated from their wives and families in China.

The poems are a vivid fragment of Chinese American history and a mirror capturing an image of that past. Let us collectively examine that image and contemplate its meaning.

The boat transporting immigrants to and from San Francisco harbor.

En route to Gam Saan, Golden Mountain.

TRANSLATORS' NOTE

In translating the following poems and interviews, we have chosen to stay as close to the original meaning as possible. A word for word literal translation would have been unfeasible in light of the fact that we are dealing with two distinctly different languages, both of which possess their own inherent idiosyncratic differences. So often there are Chinese characters for which there seemingly are no satisfactory English substitutes. In these instances, we have exercised our judgment in selecting the word or words we believe best fulfill the author's intent as well as meaning.

The act of interpretation itself implies creation and the reader should bear in mind that the process of poetic translation must involve a certain compromise. While these poems express the thoughts of the individuals who wrote them, they are not reiterations of their original literal forms. The form is oftentimes compromised in order to retain the content, which we for historic reasons feel is our first priority. We do not claim adherence to the poets' original meters or rhyme-schemes. By imitating the poetic structure, we feel an injustice to the meaning of the poem would have been committed.

It should also be noted that the Chinese terms are transliterated in the Hanzi Pinyin system. Pronunciations are approximately the same as corresponding letters in the English alphabet with the following major distinctions: vowels=Italian or Spanish values; b=*sp*in; c=i*ts*; d=s*t*em; g=s*k*y; q=*ch*urch; r=plea*s*ure with a strong mixture of r; x=*h*ouse quickly followed by hou*s*e; z=tha*t's* all; zh=Italian *c*ielo. However, in transcribing the interviews, the majority of which were conducted in Cantonese, we decided to retain the Cantonese spelling of Chinese names and terms in order to give the printed interviews a more true-to-life flavor.

—Him Mark Lai
Genny Lim

THE VOYAGE
poems 1-11

遠涉重洋

1

[1] One 'li' is approximately one third of a mile.

The sea-scape resembles lichen twisting and
    turning for a thousand *li*.[1]
There is no shore to land and it is difficult to
    walk.
With a gentle breeze I arrived at the city
    thinking all would be so.
At ease, how was one to know he was to live in a
    wooden building?

2

[2] The colloquial name given to Angel Island by the Cantonese immigrants.

Because my house had bare walls, I began
    rushing all about.
The waves are happy, laughing "Ha-ha!"
When I arrived on Island,[2] I heard I was
    forbidden to land.
I could do nothing but frown and feel angry
    at heaven.

3

[3] i.e., the rigors of travel.

As a rule, a person is twenty before he starts
    making a living.
Family circumstances have forced me to
    experience wind and dust.[3]
The heartless months and years seem bent on
    defeating me.
It is a pity that time quickly ages one.

1

水景如苔千里曲，

陸路無涯[1]路步難。

平風到埠心如是，

安樂誰知住木樓。

1 余本作"崖"

2

家徒壁立[1]始奔波，

浪聲歡同笑呵呵。

埃崙念到聞禁往，

無非皺額奈天[1]何。

1 舊金山週報作"天"

3

生平廿載始謀生，

家計逼我歷風塵。

無情歲月偏負我，

可惜[1]光陰易邁人。

1 原作"省"

4

The gold and silver of America is very
    appealing.
Jabbing an awl into the thigh[4] in search of
    glory,
I embarked on the journey.
Not only are my one-thousand pieces of gold
    already depleted, but
My countenance is blackened. It is surely for
    the sake of the family.

5

Four days before the Qiqiao Festival,[5]
I boarded the steamship for America.
Time flew like a shooting arrow.
Already, a cool autumn has passed.
Counting on my fingers, several months have
    elapsed.
Still I am at the beginning of the road.
I have yet to be interrogated.
My heart is nervous with anticipation.

[4] Su Qin (? - 317 B.C.), a scholar during the period of the Warring States (403 - 221 B.C.), was unsuccessful in gaining a post in the courts upon finishing his studies. Returning home, the contempt of his family drove him to study harder. To keep awake at night, he would hold an awl over a thigh so that as he became drowsy, his hand would drop, jabbing the awl into his flesh. Later, Su Qin became the prime minister to six states concurrently. The expression, thus, means to make a determined effort.

[5] Better known as the "Festival of the Seventh Day of the Seventh Moon," the Qiqiao Festival is widely celebrated among the Cantonese. As the legend of the Cowherd (Niulang) and the Weaver Maiden (Zhinu) is told, the Weaver Maiden in heaven one day fell in love with a mortal Cowherd. After their marriage, her loom which once wove garments for the gods fell silent. Angered by her dereliction of duty, the gods ordered her back to work. She was separated from the Cowherd by the Silver Stream or Milky Way, with the Cowherd, in the Constellation Aquila and she, across the Heavenly River in the Constellation Lyra. The couple was allowed to meet only once a year on the seventh day of the seventh moon, when the Silver Stream is spanned by a bridge of magpies. On this day, maidens display toys, figurines, artificial fruits and flowers, embroidery and other examples of their handiwork, so that men can judge their skills. It is also customary for girls to worship and make offerings of fruits to the gods.

4

美洲金銀實可愛，
錐股求榮動程來。
不第千金曾用盡，
犂黑面目爲家哉。

1 原作 "椎"

5

乞巧少四日，
搭輪來美洲。
光陰似箭射，
又已過涼秋。
屈指經數月，
尚在此路頭。
至今未曾審，
懸望心悠悠。

6

[6] A district in the Pearl River Delta, Xiangshan is the birth place of Sun Yat-sen (Sun Zhongshan, 1866 - 1925). After his death in 1925, the district name was changed to Zhongshan in Sun's memory.

Everyone says travelling to North America is
    a pleasure.
I suffered misery on the ship and sadness in
    the wooden building.
After several interrogations, still I am not
    done.
I sigh because my compatriots are being
    forceably detained.

By One from Xiangshan[6]

7

[7] See note 5.

[8] A Cantonese colloquial term for Westerner.

Originally, I had intended to come to
    America last year.
Lack of money delayed me until early
    autumn.
It was on the day that the Weaver Maiden
    met the Cowherd[7]
That I took passage on the *President Lincoln*.
I ate wind and tasted waves for more than
    twenty days.
Fortunately, I arrived safely on the American
    continent.
I thought I could land in a few days.
How was I to know I would become a
    prisoner suffering in the wooden building?
The barbarians'[8] abuse is really difficult to
    take.
When my family's circumstances stir my
    emotions, a double stream of tears flow.
I only wish I can land in San Francisco soon,
Thus sparing me this additional sorrow here.

6

北遊咸道樂悠悠，
船中苦楚木樓愁。
數次審查猶未了，
太息[1]同胞被逼留。

　　　　香山人題

1 余本作"惜"

7

本擬舊歲來美洲，
洋蚨迫阻到初秋。
織女會牛郎哥日，
乃搭林肯總統舟。
餐風嘗浪廿餘日，
幸得平安抵美洲。
以為數日可上埠，
點知苦困木樓囚。
番奴苛待真難受，
感觸家境淚雙流。
但願早登三藩市，
免在此間倍添愁。

8

Instead of remaining a citizen of China, I
    willingly became an ox.
I intended to come to America to earn a
    living.
The Western styled buildings are lofty; but I
    have not the luck to live in them.
How was anyone to know that my dwelling
    place would be a prison?

9

I used to admire the land of the Flowery
    Flag[9] as a country of abundance.
I immediately raised money and started my
    journey.
For over a month, I have experienced enough
    winds and waves.
Now on an extended sojourn in jail, I am
    subject to the ordeals of prison life.
I look up and see Oakland so close by.
I wish to go back to my motherland to carry
    the farmer's hoe.
Discontent fills my belly and it is difficult for
    me to sleep.
I just write these few lines to express what is
    on my mind.

[9] A Cantonese colloquial term for the United States.

8

國民不爲甘爲牛，
意至美洲作營謀。
洋樓高聳無緣住，
誰知棲所是監牢？

9

夙慕花旗幾優哉，
即時籌款動程來。
風波閱月已歷盡。
監牢居所受災磨。
仰望屋崙相咫尺，
願回祖國負耕鋤。
滿腹牢騷難寢寐，
聊書數句表心裁。

10

Poem by One Named Xu From Xiangshan Encouraging the Traveler

[10]See note 9.

[11]From "Tangong," a chapter in the 'Book of Rites': Confucius was passing Mt. Tai and saw a woman weeping and wailing at a grave. Confucius asked one of his disciples to ask why she was wailing so sadly. She said, "My father-in-law and my husband were killed by tigers. Now my son is also killed by a tiger." Confucius asked why she didn't leave this dangerous place. She replied that it was because there is no oppressive rule here. Confucius remarked, "Oppressive rule is surely fiercer than any tiger."

Just talk about going to the land of the
    Flowery Flag[10] and my countenance fills
    with happiness.
Not without hard work were 1,000 pieces of
    gold dug up and gathered together.
There were words of farewell to the parents,
    but the throat choked up first.
There were many feelings, many tears flowing
    face to face, when parting with the wife.

Waves big as mountains often astonished this
    traveller.
With laws harsh as tigers,[11] I had a taste of all
    the barbarities.
Do not forget this day when you land ashore.
Push yourself ahead and do not be lazy or
    idle.

11

[12]Also known as Taozhugong, a wealthy merchant who lived during the 5th century, B.C. His name is symbolic of wealth. Taozhugong was also known as Fan Li, a minister who once served King Goujian of the state of Yue. After successfully aiding the King to defeat the enemy state of Wu, Fan resigned from his post to become a merchant.

I think back on the past when I had not
    experienced hardship.
I resolved to go and seek Taogong.[12]
The months and years are wasted and still it
    has not ended.
Up to now, I am still trapped on a lonely
    island.

10

香山許生勉客題

說去花旗喜溢顏，
千金羅掘不辭艱。
親離有話喉先哽[1]，
妻別多情淚對潸。

浪大如山頻駭客，
政苛似虎備嘗蠻。
毋忘此日君登岸，
發奮前程莫懶閒。

[1] 太平洋週報作 "梗"

11

憶昔當年苦未從，
堅心出外覓陶公。
歲月蹉跎仍未了，
至今猶困島孤中。

THE VOYAGE

(Note: Most of the oral interviews were conducted in Chinese. Translations from the transcriptions were kept as literal as possible in order to retain the original flavor, even though this sometimes resulted in non-idiomatic terms and phrases in English. It should be kept in mind that the words in these accounts describe events through the subject's eyes. Frequently, misinterpretations of actions do occur due to language and cultural barriers, as well as the subject's own state of mind.)

They told me that anyone who comes to *Gam Saan*[1] will make money fast and go home a rich man. Anyone who comes to America is well respected in China. My family pushed me to come. They wanted me to make a better living. They couldn't send my older brother because he was too old to match the age of my uncle's paper son.[2] I studied (coaching papers) for a whole summer at school. It included many, many generations. I had to remember everyone's name, the birthday, and if they passed away, when. And you had to know the different points of the village, what it looked like. I remember I had an English cap that we picked up in Hong Kong and inside the cap, my father hid some coaching notes, so that once in awhile, I could refresh my memory. But I never had a

chance to look at them, because you're among people all the time and you don't trust anyone. There was no private place where I could be alone to study them. One time, they were playing catch with my cap and they didn't understand why I was so upset. I was scared."

Mr. Wong, age 12 in 1933

[1] "Golden Mountain," the colloquial Chinese term for the United States, particularly California.
[2] An immigrant who tries to enter the country on false claims that he is the alleged offspring of a citizen or merchant.

I was forced to come to America. I had never seen my husband before. My mother matched me in marriage so that I could bring the family over later. I had a passport to come when I was 16, but I didn't come until I was 23 when the Japanese attacked. Most of us then came as daughters of citizens or wives of businessmen. Other wives weren't allowed to come. I came as a granddaughter of a citizen. The papers had been purchased for me."

Mrs. Chan, age 23 in 1939

The Japanese took *Gwongjau*[3] and the country went to pieces. We did not want our communication lines abroad cut, which would have meant no more remittances from my father in America; we would have starved to death. So I wrote father to make arrangements for me to come to America. First, we escaped to Macao by sampan, my mother, aunt and others included. I stayed in Macao for three to four months before going to America through Hong Kong. At that time, we did not have to go through the American consulate in Hong Kong. Fathers here sent affidavits to Hong Kong. With the affidavit, you can buy a passage ticket. Before a son or daughter comes, the father must prepare coaching information to send them, which includes the family tree, descriptions of the village and living quarters, etc. But it can be very tricky, especially when they don't ask the essentials, but instead ask questions such as: Is there a clock? Who is in the family photos? So if they want to trip you, they can.

"There were coaching specialists in San Francisco who pointed out the important questions and details. Sample standard questions were for sale. When you received the coaching information, you calculated how long it would take to memorize it and worked your departure date around that. Many took the papers on board the ship, but as soon as they approached Hawaii, it was torn to pieces and thrown overboard or flushed."

Mr. Dea, age 26 in 1939

[3]Cantonese pronunciation of Guangzhou.

My father was here in the late 1890's. After he died in an accident, my uncle bought a merchant's son's paper for me to come to America. All the papers then were false and cost $100 per year of age. I was actually 17, but the paper said 19. After I got here, I found out that when an elder wishes to bring a younger relative over from China, he must go make contact at such places as Hip Sing Chong and buy papers for the closest age. He pays a deposit and the balance after the immigrant has landed. If he can't land, you just lose the passage cost and get the deposit back. If court fees are needed to land the immigrant, the seller of the papers must foot it. At that time, there were few court battles. Later, when the immigration laws became stricter, the applicant and seller shared the court costs fifty-fifty and the paper was paid for in full regardless of the results. If you're deported, it's your own bad luck.

"Coming to the Flowery Flag,[4] I stopped over in Hong Kong for one month and stayed at Wing Chong's, a *gam saan jong*[5] run by fellow villagers from *Wong Leung Dou*.[6] It took me a month, because first, I had to go to the Consulate's for papers, then to the doctor's to be examined for trachoma. Often, they can't see you right there and then, so you have to make an appointment and come back. Then maybe, your eyes aren't okay and you have to correct them. If they're okay, the doctor gives you the necessary papers and you go buy passage tickets next. They might not have seats when you want them, so you end up waiting again. Wing Chong's still operating now, helping people buy passage tickets, handling mail and remittances, helping travellers to get to the Flowery Flag, and putting up guarantees for aliens from America visiting Hong Kong."[7]

Mr. Tom, age 17 in 1921

[4]Land of the Flowery Flag is a Cantonese collo-
quial term for the United States.
[5]Literally, "Golden Mountain Firm." An export-
import firm doing business between the Americas
and China. The main firm is usually in Hong Kong,
with associated firms in large Chinese overseas
communities as well as in China. The firms handle
remittances and correspondence of overseas
Chinese, provide hostel facilities for emigrants
and returning immigrants, help to process paper
work as well as booking passage for emigrants,
and act as a middleman for the sale of immigration
"slots."
[6]Cantonese pronunciation of Huangliang Du, an
area formerly part of the Zhongshan district. Now,
it is a separate district, Doumen.
[7]As of 1977, when Mr. Tom was interviewed.

When we got off the boat at the San Francisco pier, we got into a little boat that took us to Angel Island, a group of about 20-odd people, all new arrivals. The first impression I got was, 'Really, it's not too bad.' At least much better than our village, what with the green grass, flowers on a hill, and a hospital there. The wooden building was not too bad either. When we got into the dormitory, the so-called Self-Governing Organization had a reception for us and the older people there made some sort of speeches to explain a little about life there. So then, I think I slept on the middle deck of the bunk beds. They had three decks, I think. Like the other high school kids from Toishan,[8] I got used to the dormitory life. So I didn't feel too bad under those circumstances."

Mr. G. Lee, age 20 in 1930

[8]Cantonese pronunciation of Taishan, one of the districts in Sze Yup.

I was a refugee in Hong Kong when the Japanese invaded. Things were so confused then, my husband decided to send for us for the sake of our son's future. We had our physical examinations in Hong Kong, where we were examined for trachoma and vaccinated for small-pox. My son had trachoma and had to have medical treatment. There wasn't much treatment involved. They scraped the eye and put ice on it afterwards. It was pretty expensive and he had to go a couple of times. We boarded the *President Pierce* and on arrival at San Francisco, transferred to a little motor launch to go next to the Island. Some people on the motor boat got pretty seasick. When we docked, there was an investigator looking for opium and jewelry. He asked to see our handbags and we let him. They then searched our luggage aboard ship. They warned you that if they found any jewelry, they would fine you. They just didn't want anyone to profit by selling any."

Mrs. Woo, age 23 in 1940

Father couldn't make a living in China and our relatives looked down at him, so he went to Hong Kong and worked at a *gam saan jong*. Later, he was smuggled aboard a ship and came to the United States. He changed to treaty merchant status[9] and returned to China when I was about 18. He reported two sons, and since I was too old to use these slots, they were given to two others. Later, when I was 25 and married, my father bought a citizen's son's paper for me to come to the U.S. It cost him $2,000, with $500 down. If I was unable to land, the $500 would have been forfeited to the seller. The paper was for someone in a neighboring village, so I visited it to familiarize myself with the place. I stayed at a *gam saan jong*, owned by Sze Yup[10] people for a month waiting for a favorable decision from the U.S. The firm helped me with the paperwork and booking passage. I finally took the Japanese ship, *Siberia*. I was not used to the wind and waves and was seasick in bed the entire voyage. I stayed in the steerage and slept on a canvas cot. We had to use sea water to wash ourselves. When we arrived at Yokohama and Nagasaki, the Japanese ordered all passengers, white and yellow alike, to strip for a physical examination. Urine was examined and temperatures taken. We Chinese took delight in seeing whites having to be examined, knowing they required Chinese to be examined before entering the U.S."

Mr. S. Low, age 25 in 1922

[9]Merchants as defined by treaty are exempted from the provisions of the exclusion laws.
[10]Four districts southwest of the Pearl River delta: Enping, Kaiping, Taishan, Xinhui.

I said I was coming to teach, but actually I wanted to come to make a better living. In Hong Kong, I used connections at the Consulate's office to come as a teacher. They tested me on general knowledge and sciences before giving me permission to come."

Mr. Chew, age 32 in 1923

My husband was a citizen, but when they did not allow wives of citizens to come, he changed to merchant status so that I could come."

Mrs. Fong, age 22 in 1922

At the time, I was a school teacher in my village. I had just finished a three-day examination at the end of the school semester. My husband had been in business for over ten years here. He had an attorney prepare my papers. They had already made our ship reservations, so once I arrived in Hong Kong it was very easy to continue on to America. Aboard the ship, we stayed in a room with two sets of bunks. My son and myself occupying one set, another woman and her son occupying the other. Confined there, it was difficult to eat. For breakfast, I'd have two eggs. I didn't eat lunch. For dinner, I had a little vegetable with rice. The woman I shared the room with didn't eat anything the whole time. She was seasick. She wouldn't eat, she wouldn't leave her bed. Later on, I climbed on deck and walked around a bit. Her, she never got out at all, never even left the room."

Mrs. Jew, age 33 in 1922

My father had a birth certificate on file, but he didn't use it. Instead, he used a student paper since he studied at church. He paid $1,500 to a fellow villager who had reported he had four sons in order to buy entry papers for me. I came over with one of the 'brothers.'

Another one had already been admitted into the country. When they interviewed the two younger brothers, the facts were conflicting. That's why I stayed there three and a half months. I had to appeal the decision. After leaving the village, I went to Hong Kong and stayed at a *gam saan jong* owned by people named Quan. I stayed there ten days to take care of the paper work for passage. At that time all I knew was that *gam saan haak*[11] who came back were always rich. They never told me about confinement on Angel Island. That's why people spent all their money to get here. They'd spend up to $1,500 to buy papers to come, thinking in a year or two they'd make it all back. There were some people who were deported. I heard that some of them committed suicide aboard the ship."

Mr. Quan, age 16 in 1913

[11] Literally, "Traveller to the Golden Mountain." A colloquial term for an emigrant to the United States.

My father was born here. I was born in Sunwui.[12] A *gam saan jong* owned by people who knew my family helped me arrange passage, so I didn't have to leave the village until everything was ready. I only stayed at *gam saan jong* for a few days. In those days, new immigrants from fellow villages could have room and board free for a few days. They made the deficit up by attracting returning Chinese from the United States, who were charged higher prices for room and board. I'm Chinese but I took a Japanese ship. In 1929 there was a meningitis epidemic in Shanghai. The Japanese refused to sell third class passage for fear the disease might spread in the crowded quarters. Only first and second class passage were available. Every week, we could be called upon to line up for a physical examination. The whites on board were forced to line up on deck, but not the Chinese. Perhaps the Japanese treated the Chinese better then because they wanted us to book passage on Japanese ships."

Mr. Lew, age 19 in 1929

[12] Cantonese pronunciation of Xinhui, one of the Sze Yap districts.

In 1936 I came on the *President Hoover*. We docked around noon, but only returning residents went ashore. New arrivals stayed on the ship overnight. What a pitiful night that was! Why? Because all our baggage had been taken by the ship's crew so we had no blankets or sheets. All of us were cold throughout the night. The next morning at eight or nine, they took us over to Angel Island on a steamer. After disembarking, we walked up the hill to the detention building carrying only a few necessities. The rest of our luggage was left in a warehouse near the wharf."

Mr. Leung, age 24 in 1936

From our village I took a small steamer to Hong Kong, where I stayed for two or three months at the Bank of

Holland. I had relatives who worked there. During the day, the space upstairs was used for offices. At night, they put out beds for us. On hot nights, we slept out on the balconies. There were many people rushing to come to *Gam Saan* because they were afraid the immigration laws might change and not permit them to come at all. So they used 'black' money[13] to book passage quickly. it was so bad. Same as the black market. They said it was easier to land if you went first class, but there were no tickets left, so I was forced to come by steerage. I even had a Western suit made for first class, which I didn't need after all. In steerage there were 100 or more men. We slept in bunk beds with luggage underneath."

Mr. S. Tong, age 17 in 1921

[13] Bribery.

The law at that time was to bar Chinese from coming and if there was any way that they could bar Chinese, they would do it. *Gon fai chung* (liver fluke) is one thing; alleged paper is another thing. And then people talk about *luk yi*. Well, what is *luk yi*? Those are the immigration officials who come and arrest Chinese and after *luk yi* come, we don't see the Chinese person anymore and that's why we always call *luk yi, luk yi,* and it didn't originally mean police department. It's the immigration officials that wear the green garments. They come and *laai ngo dei* (arrest us). See, those are the *luk yi*."

Minister's son, 1923

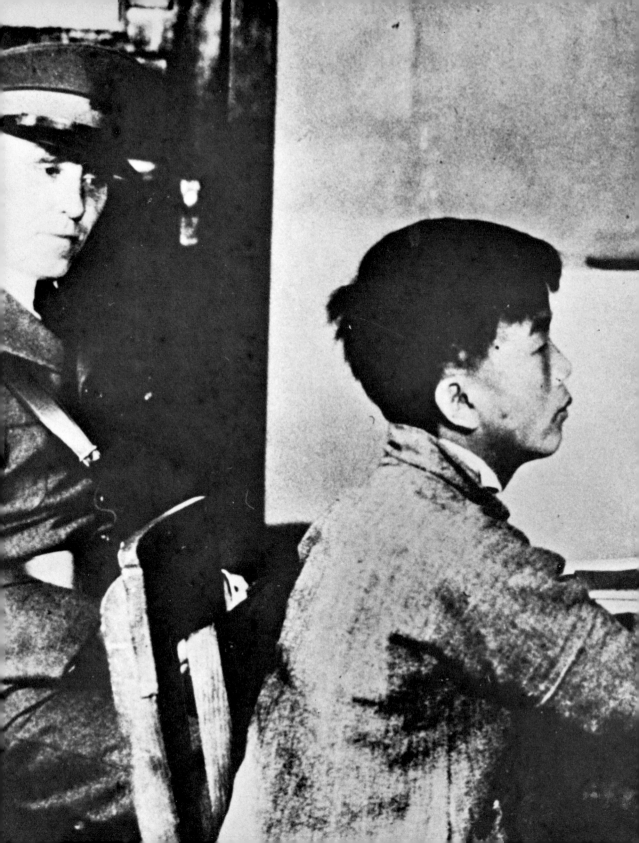

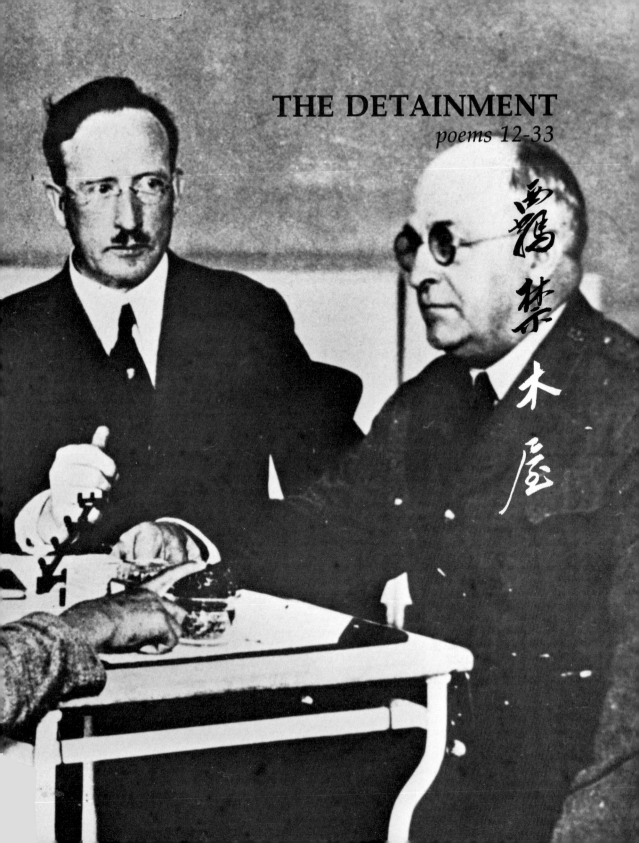

THE DETAINMENT

poems 12-33

12

Today is the last day of winter,
Tomorrow morning is the vernal equinox.
One year's prospects have changed to another.
Sadness kills the person in the wooden
    building.

13

Random Thoughts Deep at Night

[13]More commonly "Yee" in the United States

[14]A district southwest of the Pearl River Delta. The largest percentage of Chinese in continental U.S. and Canada came from this district.

In the quiet of night, I heard, faintly, the
    whistling of wind.
The forms and shadows saddened me; upon
    seeing the landscape, I composed a poem.
The floating clouds, the fog, darken the sky.
The moon shines faintly as the insects chirp.
Grief and bitterness entwined are heaven sent.
The sad person sits alone, leaning by a window.

Written by Yu[13] of Taishan[14]

14

Random Thoughts at Mid-Autumn Festival[15]

[15]The Mid-Autumn Festival is one of the major traditional festivals celebrated by the entire Chinese family together.

The night is cool as I lie stiff on the steel bunk.
Before the window the moon lady shines on me.
Bored, I get up and stand beneath the cold
    window.
Sadly, I count the time that's elapsed.
It is already mid-autumn.
We should all honor and enjoy her.
But I have not prepared even the most trifling
    gift and I feel embarrassed.

12

今日爲冬末，
明朝是春分。
交替兩年景，
愁煞木樓人。

13　　深夜偶感

夜靜微聞風嘯聲，
形影傷情見景詠。
雲霧潺潺也暗天，
蟲聲唧唧月微明。
悲苦相連天相遣，
愁人獨坐倚窗邊。
　　　　台山余題

1 原作 "椅"

14　中秋偶感

夜涼僵臥鐵床中，
窗前月姊透照儂。
悶來起立寒窗下，
愁把時計已秋中。
吾儕也應同敬賞，
菲儀無備亦羞容。

15

[16]This poem imitates the "Mulan Ci" ("Poem of Mulan"), which some judge to be a work dating back to the 6th century, A.D.

The insects chirp outside the four walls.[16]
The inmates often sigh.
Thinking of affairs back home,
Unconscious tears wet my lapel.

16

[17]See note 2.

Depressed from living on Island,[17] I sought the
    Sleeping Village.
The uncertain future altogether wounds my
    spirit.
When I see my old country fraught with chaos,
I, a drifting leaf, become doubly saddened.

17

My belly is so full of discontent it is really
    difficult to relax.
I can only worry silently to myself.
At times I gaze at the cloud- and fog-
    enshrouded mountain-front.
It only deepens my sadness.

15

四壁蟲唧唧，
居人多歎息。
思及家中事，
不覺淚沾滴[1]。

1 余本作"襟"

16

悶處埃崙尋睡鄉，
前途渺渺總神傷。
眼看故國危變亂，
一葉飄零倍感長。

17

牢騷滿腹甚難休，
默默沉沉祇自憂。
時望山前雲霧鎖，
恰似更加一點愁。

[18]Wu Yuan (? - 485 B.C.) or Wu Zixu was the son of a high official serving the King of Chu (a state in the central Yangzi River basin and the upper and middle Huai River basin). His father fell into the king's disfavor and was killed together with his family. Wu Zixu, however, fled to the state of Wu (in the present Jiangsu province). Upon arrival, he had only a flute, which he played in the market place to beg for food. Later, Wu Zixu became an important official serving the Wu king and led an army to defeat the state of Chu. His victorious legions entered the Chu capital in 506 B.C., whereupon Wu Zixu dug up the corpse of the former king and whipped it 300 times.

[19]See note 2.

[20]King Wen (ca. 12th century, B.C.), founder of the Zhou state, was held captive at Youli because the last Shang king, Zhou (1154 - 1122 B.C., different Chinese character from the preceding), regarded him as a potential threat to Shang rule. His son, King Wu (1134 - 1115 B.C.), later did defeat the Shang and establish the Zhou dynasty (1122 - 249 B.C.).

[21]This idea is taken from a proverb which alludes to crimes so numerous they will not even fit on slips made from all the bamboo in the Zhongnan mountains. The ancient Chinese often wrote on bamboo slips.

18

Sadly, I listen to the sounds of insects and
　　angry surf.
The harsh laws pile layer upon layer; how
　　can I dissipate my hatred?
Drifting in as a traveller, I met with this
　　calamity.
It is more miserable than owning only a flute
　　in the marketplace of Wu.[18]

19

Living on Island[19] away from home elicits a
　　hundred feelings.
My chest is filled with a sadness and anger I
　　cannot bear to explain.
Night and day, I sit passively and listlessly.
Fortunately, I have a novel as my companion.

20

Imprisonment at Youli,[20] when will it end?
Fur and linen garments have been exchanged;
　　it is already another autumn.
My belly brims with discontent, too numerous
　　to inscribe on bamboo slips.[21]
Snow falls, flowers wilt, expressing sorrow
　　through the ages.

18

愁聽蟲聲與怒潮，

苛例重重恨怎消？

飄流爲客遭此劫，

慘逾吳市一枝簫。

19

旅居埃崙百感生，

滿懷悲憤不堪陳。

日夜靜坐無聊¹賴²，

幸有小說可爲朋。

20

羑里受囚何日休？

裘葛已更又一秋。

滿腹牢騷難罄竹，

雪落花殘千古愁。

21

The west wind ruffles my thin gauze clothing.
On the hill sits a tall building with a room of
    wooden planks.
I wish I could travel on a cloud far away,
    reunite with my wife and son.
When the moonlight shines on me alone, the
    nights seem even longer.
At the head of the bed there is wine and my
    heart is constantly drunk.
There is no flower beneath my pillow and
    my dreams are not sweet.
To whom can I confide my innermost
    feelings?
I rely solely on close friends to relieve my
    loneliness.

22

America has power, but not justice.
In prison, we were victimized as if we were
    guilty.
Given no opportunity to explain, it was really
    brutal.
I bow my head in reflection but there is
    nothing I can do.

21

西風吹動薄羅裳[1]，
山坐高樓板木房。
意好子娘雲欲遠，
月明偏受夜更長。
床頭有酒心常醉，
枕底無花夢不香。
一幅幽情何心寄，
全憑知己解淒涼。

1 原作 "常"

22

美有強權無公理，
囹圄吾人也罹辜。
不由分說真殘酷，
俯首回思莫奈何。

23

This place is called an island of immortals,
When, in fact, this mountain wilderness is a
    prison.
Once you see the open net, why throw
    yourself in?
It is only because of empty pockets I can do
    nothing else.

24

I, a seven foot man, am ashamed I cannot
    extend myself.
Curled up in an enclosure,[22] my movements
    are dictated by others.
Enduring a hundred humiliations, I can only
    cry in vain.
This person's tears fall, but what can the blue
    heavens do?

[22] i.e., like a worm.

25

I have infinite feelings that the ocean
    has changed into a mulberry grove.[23]
My body is detained in this building.
I cannot fly from this grassy hill,
And green waters block the hero.
Impetuously, I threw away my writing brush.
My efforts have all been in vain.
It is up to me to answer carefully.
I have no words to murmur against the east
    wind.

[23] i.e. great changes.

[24] More commonly "Yuen" in
the United States.

By Ruan[24]

23

埃崙此地為仙島[1]，
山野原來是監牢。
既望張網焉投入？
祇為囊空莫奈何。

[1] 余本作"如"

24

鬚眉七尺愧無伸，
蜷伏圈中俯仰人。
百般忍辱徒呼負，
斯人瀝[1]哭蒼天何？

[1] 原作"磨"

25

無限滄桑感，
羈身此樓中。
青山飛不去，
綠水阻英雄。
率爾投筆去，
徒勞反無功。
慎言誠在我，
無語怨東風。

阮題

61

[25]Wang Can (177 - 217 A.D.) was an official during a politically chaotic period. While a refugee in Jingzhou (in Hubei province), he composed a verse in the "fu" form, entitled, "Denglou" ("Ascending the Tower"), expressing his own unfortunate circumstances and thoughts of home.

[26]Yu Xin (513 - 581 A.D.) was an official of the Liang dynasty (502 - 557 A.D.) He was sent as an envoy to the northern state of Western Wei (535 - 557 A.D.) and was subsequently detained there. Later, he served the succeeding Northern Zhou dynasty (557 - 581 A.D.). In his later years, he composed a verse in the "fu" form, "Ai Jiangnan" ("Bewailing Jiangnan"), reflecting his longing for his native south and describing the rise and fall of the Liang dynasty.

26

My grief, like dense clouds, cannot be
    dispersed.
Whether deliberating or being melancholy
    and bored,
I constantly pace to and fro.
Wang Can ascended the tower but who
    pitied his sorrow?[25]
Lord Yu who left his country could only wail
    to himself.[26]

27

**Poem by One Named Xu, From Xiangshan,
Consoling Himself**

Over a hundred poems are on the walls.
Looking at them, they are all pining at the
    delayed progress.
What can one sad person say to another?
Unfortunate travellers everywhere wish to
    commiserate.
Gain or lose, how is one to know what is
    predestined?
Rich or poor, who is to say it is not the will
    of heaven?
Why should one complain if he is detained
    and imprisoned here?
From ancient times, heroes often were the
    first ones to face adversity.

26

愁似濃雲撥不開，
思量愁悶輒徘徊。
登樓王粲誰憐苦？
去國庾郎只自哀。

27

香山許生自慰題

壁上題詩過百篇，
看來皆是嘆迍邅。
愁人曷向愁人訴，
蹇客偏思蹇客憐。
得失豈知原有命，
富貧誰謂不由天。
此間困處何須怨，
自古英雄每厄先。

28

[27] When Confucius (551 - 479 B.C.) and his disciples were on the road between Chen and Cai (both in the present Henan province), officials of these states feared his appointment as an official in the powerful neighboring state of Chu (in the present Hubei province, extending to the middle Yangzi River basin and the upper and middle Huai River basin). Chu posed a perpetual threat to these smaller states; therefore, to prevent Confucius from proceeding on to Chu, the officials ordered troops to surround them and cut off their food supplies for several days.

The male eagle is also easy to tame.
One must be able to bend before one can
 stretch.
China experienced calamities for a thousand
 years.
Confucius was surrounded in Chen for seven
 days.[27]
Great men exhibit quality,
Scholars take pride in being themselves.
Gains and losses are entangled in my bosom.
My restlessness is a sign of self-illumination.

29

[28] See note 2.

Half way up the hill on Island,[28] in the
 building upstairs,
The imprisoned one has been separated from
 his people summer to autumn.
Three times I dreamed of returning to the
 native village.
My intestines are agitated in its nine turns by
 the false Westerner.
I have run into hard times and am uselessly
 depressed.
There are many obstacles in life but who will
 commiserate with me?
If at a later time I am allowed to land on the
 American shore,
I will toss all the miseries of this jail to the
flowing current.

28

雄鷹亦易馴，
能屈始能伸。
也歷千年劫，
曾困七日陳。
偉人多本色，
名士樂天眞。
得失縈懷抱，
心猿證悟[1]禪。

1 余本作"憬"

29

埃崙山半樓上樓，
囚困離人夏至[1]秋。
夢繞三勻歸故里，
腸迴九曲傷西歐。
時運不濟[2]空自悶，
命途多阻共誰憂？
倘得他時登美岸，
畢拋牢慘付水流。

1 余本作"自"
2 余本作"齊"

[29] According to a folk tale, the daughter of the legendary Yandi, while playing in the Eastern Sea, was drowned. Her soul changed to a bird called the "jingwei," who, resenting the fact that the ocean took her life, carried pebbles in her beak from the Western Mountains and dropped them into the ocean, hoping to fill it.

[30] Another name for Su Wu (140 - 60 B.C.), who during the Western Han dynasty (206 B.C. - 24 A.D.) was sent by the Chinese government as envoy to Xiongnu, a nomadic people north of the Chinese empire. Su Wu was detained there for 19 years, but refused to renounce his loyalty to the Han emperor.

[31] Ruan Ji (210 - 263 A.D.), a scholar during the period of the Three Kingdoms (220 - 280 A.D.), was a person who enjoyed drinking and visiting mountains and streams. Often when he reached the end of the road, he would cry bitterly before turning back.

[32] See note 6.

30

After leaping into prison, I cannot come out.
From endless sorrows, tears and blood streak.
The *jingwei*[29] bird carries gravel to fill its old
    grudge.
The migrating wild goose complains to the
    moon, mourning his harried life.
When Ziqing[30] was in distant lands, who
    pitied and inquired after him?
When Ruan Ji[31] reached the end of the road,
    he shed futile tears.
The scented grass and hidden orchids
    complain of withering and falling.
When can I be allowed to rise above as I
    please?

By Li Jingbo of Taishan District

31

There are tens of thousands of poems
    composed on these walls.
They are all cries of complaint and sadness.
The day I am rid of this prison and attain
    success,
I must remember that this chapter once
    existed.
In my daily needs, I must be frugal.
Needless extravagance leads youth to ruin.
All my compatriots should please be mindful.
Once you have some small gains, return
    home early.

By One From Xiangshan[32]

30

牢籠躍入出無能，
無任傷悲血淚橫。
精衛啣砂塡夙恨，
征鴻訴月哀頻生。
子卿絕域誰憐問？
阮籍途窮空哭行。
芳草幽蘭怨凋落，
那時方得任升騰？

台邑李鏡波題

31

壁墻題詠萬千千，
盡皆怨語及愁言。
若卸此牢升騰日，
要憶當年有個編。
日用所需宜省儉，
無爲奢侈誤青年。
幸我同胞牢緊念，
得些微利早回旋。

香山題

67

32

Imprisoned in the wooden building day after
　　day,
My freedom withheld; how can I bear to talk
　　about it?
I look to see who is happy but they only sit
　　quietly.
I am anxious and depressed and cannot fall
　　asleep.
The days are long and the bottle constantly
　　empty; my sad mood, even so, is not
　　dispelled.
Nights are long and the pillow cold; who can
　　pity my loneliness?
After experiencing such loneliness and sorrow,
Why not just return home and learn to plow
　　the fields?

32

囚困木屋天復天，
自由束縛豈堪言？
舉目誰歡惟靜坐，
關心自悶不成眠。
日永樽空愁莫解，
夜長枕冷倩誰憐？
參透箇中孤苦味，
何如歸去學耕田？

33
Inscription About a Wooden Building[33]

A building does not have to be tall; if it has
　　windows, it will be bright.
Island is not far, Angel Island.
Alas, this wooden building disrupts my
　　travelling schedule.
Paint on the four walls are green,
And green is the grass which surrounds.
It is noisy because of the many country folk,
And there are watchmen guarding during the
　　night.
To exert influence, one can use a square-
　　holed elder brother.[34]
There are children who disturb the ears,
But there are no incoherent sounds that
　　cause fatigue.
I gaze to the south at the hospital,[35]
And look to the west at the army camp.[36]
This author says, "What happiness is there in
　　this?

[33]This composition imitates the style of "Loushi Ming" ("Inscription About a Humble House") by Liu Yuxi (772 - 842 A.D.).

[34]i.e., money. The ancient Chinese coin had a square hole in the center.

[35]The writer here appears to be confused in his directions. The long axis of the barracks building runs roughly in an eastern-western direction. The occupants can see the hospital to the north from windows in the building's north wall. Looking east, the Ft. McDowell buildings can be seen. No buildings can be seen from the south wall windows which face the hillside.

[36]See note 35.

木屋銘

樓不在高，有窗則明；

島不在遠，烟治埃崙。

嗟此木屋，阻我行程。

四壁油漆綠，

週圍草色青。

喧嘩多鄉里，

守夜有巡丁。

可以施運動，孔方兄。

有孩子之亂耳，

無咕嗶之勞形。

南望醫生房，

西瞭陸軍營。

作者云，" 何樂之有？"

THE DETAINMENT

When we first arrived, we were told to put down our luggage and they pushed us towards the buildings. More than 100 of us arrived. The men had their dormitories and the women, theirs. They assigned us beds and there were white women to take care of us. When we returned from the dining hall, they locked the doors behind us. Once you're locked in, they don't bother with you. It was like being in prison. Some read newspapers or books; some knitted. There was a small fenced-in area for exercising, sunning, and ball-playing. There were windows and we could see the boats arrive daily at about 9:30 or 10 a.m. Once a week, they allowed us to walk out to the storage shed where our luggage was kept. We could write as many letters as we wanted, but they examined our letters before mailing them. The same for letters coming in. There were good friends, but there were also those who didn't get along. There were arguments and people cried when they saw others who were fortunate enough to leave, especially those of us who had been there a long time. I must have cried a bowlful during my stay at Angel island. Most of the women were Sze Yup.[14] Because I was *Lung Dou,*[15] I couldn't understand most of them. We were all in the twenties, thirties, or forties; no one older. New arrivals came every two weeks—about thirty or forty. Most left after three weeks. There were about twenty or thirty appealing their cases like me. Three or four out of every ten would end up appealing. But I was there the longest and always the one left behind."

Mrs. Chan, age 23 in 1939

[14] Four districts southwest of the Pearl River Delta: Enping, Kaiping, Taishan, Xinhui.

[15] Cantonese pronunciation of Long Du, an area in the Zhongshan district.

There was not much for us to do on the Island. In the morning, we got up and washed our faces. Afterwards, we had breakfast. After we ate, we napped or washed our own clothes. At lunch time, we had congee in a large serving bowl with some cookies. Then at night we had rice with a main dish. You picked at some of it, I picked at some of it, and that was that. We ate in a huge dining hall. After the women ate, the men ate. As the women passed, the men teased us, whistling, saying this-and-that; they were so naughty. They allowed us to go outside to the yard or even out to the dock, where there were grass and trees, tall and fan-like. The women were allowed to wander around, jump around, and stick our hands or feet into the water to fish out seaweed. Otherwise, the day would have been hard to pass."

Mrs. Chin, age 19 in 1913

When we arrived, they locked us up like criminals in compartments like the cages at the zoo. They counted us and then took us upstairs to our rooms. There were two to three rooms in the women's section, all facing the shore. Each of the rooms could fit twenty or thirty persons. The spring beds could be folded up. The main door was locked, but we could go into the other rooms from the hallway. The hall was wide, with tables and chairs where you could play dominoes. You didn't have to stay in your room during the day. You could come out into the hall. There was also an office there. We could ask questions of the white woman who took care of us at the office. One kid who had stayed for two years could speak English. He called her Mama. He was eight or nine. He translated for us. The woman even gave haircuts to the three boys staying in the women's section then. There was a back yard that was fenced in so we couldn't get out. We could hang our wash out there. It wasn't too bad. It was just that you couldn't go out. The place was very clean. There were two bathrooms and three or four stalls inside of each. The toilet doors were cut off at the bottom so they could see your feet. Maybe it was because they were afraid of people committing suicide. There were wash basins and sinks, bathtubs, hot water, toilet paper, and soap for us to use. People chatted in the hallway or in their rooms, sang for pleasure, or read books. The old-timers were familiar with one another, but they left the newcomers pretty much alone. We were Sam Yup[16] and didn't know them. When we arrived, we were kind of shy and distant, so there really wasn't much to say."

Mrs. Woo, age 23 in 1940

[16] Three districts in the suburbs of Guangzhou: Nanhai, Panyu, Shunde.

In a big hall with about twenty beds, my son slept on the top bunk, I on the bottom. There were many Japanese. They arrived and left on the launch within 24 hours. But us, we were confined inside so long. I kept thinking in my heart, 'What a worthless trip coming here! Confined all the time. It's just like being in jail!' There were all types of women living there. There were prostitutes, bad women too, who stayed on the other end of the room. They didn't come over to our side. There were some bad women there who had been confined there for two or three years. They could see that my son who was fourteen was a pretty big boy. 'Come over here, come on over and I'll give you a present!' they would urge him. After that, I followed my son everywhere! I went with him to the bathroom, wherever he went, I followed. I didn't dare let him go anywhere alone. There were not many children in the women's quarters. There was a white woman who took us for a walk on the hills weekly. I went twice on these walks. If you wanted to knit, you could, but you used what you brought along. Some of the ladies who were there for a long time finished a lot of knitting projects. If you didn't have anything, you didn't do anything. That's why in just two weeks, I was so disgusted and bored at just sitting around! There wasn't anything special about it. Day in, day out, the same thing. Every person had to be patient and tell herself, 'I'm just being delayed, it doesn't matter.' I never even bathed. I kept thinking each day that I would be ready to leave and as each day went by, I just waited. I didn't eat much, nor move around much, so I never perspired. I had no clothes to wash. Even if I had clothes to wash, I couldn't do it. There was no place to hang your laundry. And there was no place for you to write letters. There was no table, not even a chair, just a bed. I kept thinking, 'Had I known it was like this, I never would have wanted to come!' "

Mrs. Jew, age 33 in 1922

We would get up in the morning, and there was no set time for this, and have plain congee with fermented bean curd. Then, after breakfast, we could go out and exercise. The yard was open to us after breakfast and closed before dinner, which was at about five or six. After lunch, we rested, played chess or *mah jong*[17] read, or chatted. I wrote in my diary, read, or talked with others. I had books with me from China. There were some newspapers, but no magazines. Lights went out at a certain hour, about 9 p.m."

Mr. Dea, age 26 in 1939

[17]A Chinese game usually played with four persons with 144 tiles. Similar to dominoes.

Once a week, we had meetings in an open space in the barracks (about 15' x 20'). There were presentations of Cantonese opera. We used donated musical instruments. We even had men who could do female impersonations. The open space was also used for sitting, relaxing, and reading. I remember a Mr. Fong who used to give haircuts for 25 cents. He was a barber back home and he had brought all the equipment with him."

Mr. Yip, age 26 in 1921

We stayed in the dormitory most of the time. There wasn't much recreation. At most, there were one or two ping pong tables at the end of the room. There were over 100 people living there and all of us were young and wanted to play, so I never did get a chance to play. Some gambled at *mah jong* and tossing coins. Someone would roll a half dollar on the floor. The next person would try to hit it with another half dollar. If he hits it, he keeps it. If he misses, he loses a half dollar. There was also a basketball court outside open certain hours during the day, but most people read for recreation. There were at least five different newspapers from San Francisco. Day or night, there was always someone playing the phonograph at least until 12 midnight."

Mr. Ng, age 15 in 1931

I had nothing to do there. During the day, we stared at the scenery beyond the barbed wires—the sea and the sky and clouds that were separated from us. Besides listening to the birds outside the fence, we could listen to records and talk to old-timers in the barracks. Some, due to faulty responses during the interrogation and lengthy appeal procedures, had been there for years. They poured out their sorrow unceasingly. Their greatest misery stemmed from the fact that most of them had had to borrow money for their trips to America. Some mortgaged their houses; some sold their land; some had to borrow at such high interest rates that their family had to sacrifice. A few committed suicide in the detention barracks. The worst part was the toilet. It was a ditch congested with filth. It stank up the whole barracks. We slept on three tiers of canvas bunks. The blankets were so coarse that it might have been woven of wolf's hair. It was indeed a most humiliating imprisonment."

Mr. Lowe, age 16 in 1939

There was a Chinese Self-Governing Organization there that was formed to promote the welfare of newcomers. On arrival, newcomers were encouraged to join the organization for $2 or $3. Once a member, you could ask for help whenever you needed it. You could be nominated for office only if you had been told you could not land and your case was under litigation. The organization helped in this way: When someone made a mistake during the interrogation, coaching information was sneaked into Angel Island from San Francisco by Chinese kitchen helpers. The information was hidden in a newspaper and tossed to a particular officer assigned to receive the newspaper. If the guard should try to seize the message, we were all prepared to fight him. Returning upstairs, the message was given to the addressee, who in turn paid $5 to the officer who had picked up the newspaper. Once a guard did try to grab the newspaper at the upstairs gate. The Chinese cornered him and beat him until he could go nowhere. After that, he didn't dare pick on the Chinese again. We knew that when we went downstairs to eat, the guards would come to search our beds and belongings for coaching information."

Mr. Leung, age 24 in 1936

There were about 70 men and children. Most of them were in their teens or twenties. Boys who were 11 or 12 stayed in the men's barracks. When we first got there, they had fumigated the building, so we had to wait outside for three hours. At that time, because of the anti-Chinese agitation in Cuba, there were many Chinese from Cuba waiting for a ship to return to China.[18]

The windows had barbed wire. They opened the door. They watched you go into the mess hall. They locked the mess door and they watched you. No way you could get away. We played volleyball, but the courtyard was fenced all around so you couldn't run away. The Chinese organization collected membership fees

75

so they had money to buy *mah jong* sets, razors, phonograph records, Chinese chess sets, and a lot of things. They also gave haircuts. We had musical instruments we had brought from China. We formed a music club there and played every night. So Angel Island in my mind wasn't too bad. You didn't have to worry about working and food. You could even read many books."

Mr. Lee, age 21 in 1934

[18] In 1933 the Cuban government promulgated a law for nationalization of labor requiring at least 50 percent of the total wages as well as employment in all existing agricultural, commercial and industrial organizations in Cuba be assigned to and filled by native Cubans. This law was designed to eliminate alien employees in favor of native Cubans and to deprive aliens of a chance to work for a living.

There was only one guard sitting outside the door. If someone was sick, they would call someone in to look at you. In those days, we brought along our own medicines and herbs in case we became ill. There was a basin for us to wash our clothes. You'd string rope across from one bed to another to hang the wash or else you draped it over the radiator. You had to provide your own soap. Tell you though, if you left anything lying around, someone would take it. Really, it was very bad. Being young, I learned fast. After being there two weeks, you were considered *gau haak*.[19] When a new boat came in, the old-timers would steal things from the newcomers' luggage. They brought all kinds of things,

canned goods, snacks. On Angel Island, there was nothing like that to eat; only newcomers had them. Even a can of preserved fish would be stolen as they rummaged through the suitcases. Everyone lost something. When I was there, I lost things, so I stole too."

Mr. Quan, age 16 in 1913

[19] The Cantonese term for an old-timer, one who has been in the United States before and was now returning again after a visit to China.

Some old-timers set up gambling and barbershop businesses. One person detained for three years made $6,000. One day, someone stole his suitcase of money. He reported it to the authorities and it was later found in the bathroom. After that, he gave it to the authorities to keep in the safe."

Mr. Low, age 15 in 1919

There was a near riot up in the women's quarters. One woman was stealing all the soap and all the other women knew who the culprit was. It was bedlam and they sent us up there to see what it was all about. At that time, there was a baggage man who took care of all the luggage in the shed near the pier. So we went out with him and opened up all the luggage and, sure enough, there's about a dozen or twenty cakes of soap. They didn't do anything to her. After all, these women came from extreme poverty in the village and here they see all this soap, so naturally..."

Immigration interpreter, 1928

Arelative who was the chief cook there got me the job as kitchen helper. We were all hired by a private, white contractor. The cooks and kitchen helpers were all Chinese. According to a prior agreement, each meal cost the Chinese 17 cents. Twenty-five cents in those days could buy you pot roast or stew in Chinatown. Before the hearing, the steamship company paid for the meals. If you should fail and decide to appeal your case, then you paid for your own meals thereafter.

"We served rice for the morning and evening meals and congee with pork or tapioca soup with crackers for lunch on alternate days. The boss made money on the lunches. Noodles were served on Sunday. If that didn't fill you, you could always buy sandwiches at the concession. We served one large dish and one small one with the rice. The main dish included soup and the following served in turn: vermicelli and pork, dried bean curd and pork, potatoes and beef, dried greens, and fish—usually sanddab on Tuesdays and Fridays. The small dish was usually either salted fish, fermented bean curd, or hoisin [20] sauce. Nothing special was served on holidays.

"There were 33 tables in all, which seated six or eight people apiece. When I was there, there were over 700 Chinese inmates, so they had to eat in shifts. Each meal took half-an-hour. It went very fast.

We would place the food on the table before they came. Then voom, they ate and left. Everyone ate at the same place each time. Two guards accompanied the group to the dining room. They would count heads on arrival and before departure.

"We used two steamers to cook the food. When ready, the dishes were wheeled out on a cart. There were no seconds on dishes, just on rice. Many of the immigrants could eat six to seven bowls of rice at a meal. If it wasn't enough, you could fill up with the salted fish. The boss had us cook extra dishes to sell. We also steamed or warmed up dishes that immigrants brought to us. We would put them out on a cart when done and people would come to claim them.

"When we had time, we were assigned to peel potatoes or cut salted fish into chunks. The red potatoes were about two inches in diameter and the cheapest available. The Chinese cabbage were at least three or four feet long, what we would call throwaways. We always served the old bread first. It didn't come sliced or wrapped, so we had to cut it with an electric knife that was sharp enough for the hard bread. The food, although cheap, was clean. No one ever got sick because of the food. They were very conscientious about inspecting the kitchen. If they even saw a cockroach, they would fumigate.

"We ate better. The steamed rice the immigrants ate was no good, so we cooked our own rice separately. On our days off, we would go to San Francisco to buy food and liquor, which we shared.

"Every week, we each had one day off.

We would drop by Canton Flower Shop and ask if there was any coaching information to take back to the Island. There were eight of us working there, so one of us was off every day of the week. Each time we did this, we were given $5. We were prepared to be searched on return. When things got tight, we didn't try to bring in anything. We never got caught. On return, we would press a buzzer and someone would run down quickly for the message. We only did this for people we knew well, such as fellow villagers.

"There was a demonstration against the food when I was there. The reason was this: There was a Chinese Self-Governing Organization there that wanted fair treatment for the Chinese, including better food. Everyone agreed and started throwing dishes around the dining hall. The immigration people then called the Chinese Consul General, who sent a representative down to explain that the food was set by an agreement with the government. It could not be changed by the cooks. Anyway, they still thought it was our fault and wanted to beat us up. The white boss then pointed a gun at them and said, 'Whoever comes in first, gets it first.' No one dared. Soldiers were then called over from Fort Mc-Dowell and everyone was forced back upstairs. Did you know they refused to come down to the dining hall to eat for the next three days? We cooked as usual, but they refused to eat. So the boss closed the food concession that sold sandwiches and cookies to punish them.

"It was hard work, but one thing I liked about it was this: Being over there, we never got caught in the middle of *tong* fights[21] over in the city. There was one old man who never went over to San Francisco, even on his day off. He was so scared of the *tong* fights. After a year or so, he saved enough money to go home to his village."

Mr. Low, Kitchen Helper, 1923-1925

[20]A sweet and slightly spicy sauce made from soya-bean, salt, sugar, red-chili, garlic and flour, often used with meats and seafood.
[21]Known as "tong wars," these were conflicts between rival secret societies, sometimes resulting in killings and assassinations of members of rival groups.

I remember once being asked to go around and try to smooth things out after a food riot. You see, the concessionaire only received so much money from the steamship company to pay for the board of these people until they were released, sometimes for six weeks, two months, or even three months. So naturally, the company tried to pay as little as possible to the concessionaire to feed the people. This concessionaire then hired the Chinese staff and tried to think of the cheapest meal they could produce. Another problem was that the kitchen was designed for serving American food with a lot of steamers instead of *woks*.[22] So you can imagine the difficult situation. No wok to cook Chinese food. And then they would buy the cheapest grade of rice and steam it in these big steamers. So the detainees got mad and started a riot."

Immigration interpreter, 1928

[22]A deep frying pan used in Chinese cooking.

78

Whenever the bunch of us had to go downstairs to the dining hall to eat, we sounded like a thundering herd. Breakfast was served at nine. By 8:30, everyone would gather at the door, fighting to be first. Sometimes, when the guard was a few minutes late opening the door, the bad ones would kick the door and shout, 'Hey, we want to eat! Are you trying to starve us?' It was like a riot and people downstairs would think there was a revolt going on upstairs. As soon as the man opened the door, he would have to stand aside or be knocked over. It was like letting the cattle out. Speaking of it now, I'm embarrassed. Everyone rushed down for fear there wouldn't be anything left to eat or that there wouldn't be enough for the last ones. The stairs were very wide. At least eight could walk it abreast, but because of us, it was always a one way traffic. When we went down, no one could come up. When we went up, no one could do down."

Mr. Ng, age 15 in 1931

For meals, we went to the big dining hall. At the sound of the bell, we all went down together, about twenty of us in a group escorted by two guards. The melon was chopped in pieces thrown together like pig slop. The pork was in big, big chunks. Everything was thrown into a big bowl that resembled a wash tub and left there for you to eat or not as you wished. They just steamed the food till it was like a soupy stew. After looking at it, you'd lose your appetite. There was cabbage, stewed vegetables, pork, bits of stewed meat of low quality, that kind of thing. Sometimes, we would receive roast ducks and chickens from relatives in San Francisco. But you could only eat a little of it. There was no place to store it, no place to heat it up, so we heated it on top of the radiators for awhile and ate some of that."

Mrs. Jew, age 33 in 1922

When we ate, they opened the doors electrically and took us downstairs to a large dining hall. There were long tables and benches and we sat there facing each other like prisoners. They gave us a big bowl of food for so many people. There weren't too many dishes, usually just one to go with the rice: salted vegetables, black beans, red grain rice, and things like that. It was cruel. The rice was reddish and coarse, not white rice."

Mrs. Woo, age 23 in 1940

Because there had not been enough food for us in China, I enjoyed the meals on Angel Island. Meals were always served on time. There were one or two old-timers who knew some English and had contact with the white people downstairs. They would help in the white men's mess hall and bring us back sandwiches, apples, oranges, and such foods."

Mr. Lee, age 21 in 1934

There were two meals a day. It was ordinary food, with fish and meat, and usually seasonal vegetables. The cooking skills were too inferior and the food was difficult to swallow. In addition, new Chinese arrivals were not used to eating refrigerated meats and many chose to remain half-hungry."

Mr. Ma, age 17 in 1922

We had rice to eat, but we thought they were feeding us left-overs. Those women there said, 'They're giving us left-overs, ox-tail and the likes all mixed together for us to eat!' But actually, it was stew. I don't remember whether it was tasty or not. As children, we ate anything when we were hungry."

Mrs. Jew, age 19 in 1924

For meals, we had lima beans and pork knuckles, seaweed and dried shrimps, congee, bean curd and pork, etc. There was no beef; all were cheap cuts, such as knuckles and tripe. No variety, always the same thing. If you gave them 25 cents, you could have a steak. On the ship, we had three eggs, toast, mush, and coffee for ten cents. Only those who had been on Angel Island for some time knew there were such things as steaks. The newcomers never even heard of such things."

Mr. Yip, age 26 in 1921

My father, on the way over in the boat, always liked to tell stories, some funny incident. He would try it out on me first and see if I understood and laughed. We used to bring toys. I remember once we had a book given to us by the Children's Aid Society and instead of how to make kites, this book showed how to fold paper into birds and airplanes and I remember bringing that over and leaving it with them so they could make their own toys out of paper. The Chinese boys would tell me how they kept score 'kicking the shuttlecock,' and then I would tell them how to play marbles, jacks, hopscotch and things like that. I was eight or nine years old and went (to Angel Island) only in the later years when they allowed more visitors."

Minister's son, 1923

When the Chinese were confined over there, there really was no date that they could expect to be released, so that it really was a very tedious, frustrating, and discouraging time for them. Now, the Immigration Department did have a so-called Christian service which permitted the Methodist Church to send a deaconess over to establish an office. The person that was working most consistently was a deaconess by the name of Katharine Maurer. She usually gathered toys and different things for the kids and made life a little more enjoyable for them. And she also tried to teach them about the Bible and different things like that. The deaconess kind of designated the YMCA as their community contact. One reason was that there was very little contact between the Chinatown YMCA and other Chinatown organizations because it was Christian and there were a lot of anti-Christian feelings within the community in the twenties. The YMCA in those years was not an 'in' organization.[23] What the Immigration feared the most was that the Chinese would send in Chinese newspapers with markings (coaching notes). That's what they wanted to keep out and that's the thing that the YMCA stayed clear of. We didn't make personal contacts or talk about personal matters whatsoever. When we went over, we usually brought a minister with us and some recreational materials: volleyball, soccer, and so on. We taught them the different games and the preacher would give a talk on Christianity.

"The YMCA also helped to organize their activities organization, which was called *Ji Ji Wui* (Self-Governing Organization). They collected their own fees and wrote us to order for them certain supplies and things like that.

"We talked to them in small groups of boys, then young men, then women, about what they should expect when they landed in Chinatown, and where they should go. We referred them to the churches; they all had night schools or English schools and we told them how important that was. When we finished speaking, they urged us to continue and asked us to come back again. Kind of boring over at the Island, you know.

"The men seemed to be depressed all the time because there was no way they could know when their case would come up for examination and when they would be released. If you were in jail, you would at least know when you would be out; but there, you didn't."

YMCA Director, 1939

[23]Since the 1850's, Protestant missionaries have worked among the Chinese in California. Their relations with the Chinese were amicable; however, their doctrinaire position which excluded the co-existence of Chinese traditional religious beliefs with Christianity, as well as their condescending attitude toward traditional Chinese culture, caused most Chinese, especially China-born, to reject Christianity. Until a more Westernized generation grew in number during the second quarter of the twentieth century, social intercourse between Christian and non-Christian organizations were limited, and the Christian organizations remained outside the Chinatown traditional organizational structure.

THE WEAK SHALL CONQUER

poems 34-46

團 強 雪 恥

34

For what reason must I sit in jail?
It is only because my country is weak and
    my family poor.
My parents wait at the door but there is no
    news.
My wife and child wrap themselves in quilt,
    sighing with loneliness.
Even if my petition is approved and I can
    enter the country,
When can I return to the Mountains of Tang[37]
    with a full load?
From ancient times, those who venture out
    usually become worthless.
How many people ever return from battles?

35

Leaving behind my writing brush and
    removing my sword, I came to America.
Who was to know two streams of tears would
    flow upon arriving here?
If there comes a day when I will have
    attained my ambition and become
    successful,
I will certainly behead the barbarians and
    spare not a single blade of grass.

34

爲乜來由要坐監？
祇緣國弱與家貧。
椿萱[1]倚門無消息，
妻兒擁被歎孤單。
縱然批准能上埠，
何日滿載返唐山？
自古出門多變賤。
從來征戰幾人還？

1 舊金山週報作 "楦"

35

留筆除劍到美洲，
誰知到此淚雙流？
倘若得志成功日，
定斬胡人草不留。

[38]More commonly "Wong" in the United States.

[39]The district administrative center of Xiangshan (Shiqi).

[40]The colloquial Chinese name for California.

[41]See note 2.

[42]The town of Shiqi, which is the name of the administrative center for the Xiangshan (later renamed Zhongshan) district.

[43]The year 1924.

36

I am a member of the Huang[38] clan from
    Xiangcheng.[39]
I threw away my writing brush and pushed
    forward, journeying to the capital of the
    U.S.
I bought an oar and arrived in the land of the
    Golden Mountain.[40]
Who was to know they would banish me to
    Island?[41]
If my country had contrived to make herself
    strong, this never would have happened.
Then when the ship had docked, we could
    have gone directly ashore.

    **Idle Brush-Strokes of a Wanderer from the Town of
        Iron** [42]
    Dawn of the 24th, in the 13th Year of the Republic[43]

37

Just now the five nationalities in China have
    become one family,[44]
But the powers still have not yet recognized
    our China,
Primarily because foreign debts were piling
    up,
The foreigners pushed to control finances
    and to seize power.

36

黃家子弟本香城，
挺身投筆赴美京。
買棹[1]到了金山地，
誰知撥我過埃崙。
我國圖強無此樣，
船泊岸邊直可登。

民國十三廿肆晨
逍遙子鐵城閒筆

1 原作 "掉"

37

方今五族爲一家，
列強未認我中華。
究因外債頻頻隔，
逼監財政把權拿。

38

Being idle in the wooden building, I opened
    a window.
The morning breeze and bright moon lingered
    together.
I reminisce the native village far away, cut off
    by clouds and mountains.
On the little island the wailing of cold, wild
    geese can be faintly heard.
The hero who has lost his way can talk
    meaninglessly of the sword.
The poet at the end of the road can only
    ascend a tower.
One should know that when the country is
    weak, the people's spirit dies.
Why else do we come to this place to be
    imprisoned?

39

Twice I have passed through the blue ocean,
    experienced the wind and dust of journey.
Confinement in the wooden building has
    pained me doubly.
With a weak country, we must all join
    together in urgent effort.
It depends on all of us together to roll back
    the wild wave.[45]

[45] Quotation from an essay by Han Yu (768 - 824 A.D.), a scholar and official during the Tang dynasty (618 - 907 A.D.). "To return the violent wave that had fallen," i.e., to make an effort to restore declined fortunes.

38

木屋閒來把窗開，
曉風明月共徘徊。
故鄉遠憶雲山斷，
小島微聞寒雁哀。
失路英雄空說劍，
窮途騷士且登台。
應知國弱人心死，
何事囚困此處來？

39

兩經滄海歷風塵，
木屋羈留倍痛深。
國弱亟當齊努力，
狂瀾待挽仗同羣。

1 余本作"極"

[46] Part of the territory of the northeast provinces of China (Manchuria) which were lost to Japan in 1931 - 1932.

[47] The lower Yellow River Valley, where Chinese civilization had its beginnings.

[48] Changshan refers to Yan Gaoqing (? - 756 A.D.), an official of the Tang dynasty (618 - 917 A.D.). During the An Lushan Rebellion (755 - 760 A.D.), Yan led an army to fight the rebels. He was defeated and captured. All during the execution, he continued to revile the enemy.

[49] Zu Di (266 - 321 A.D.) was a general during the Western Jin dynasty (265 - 316 A.D.). When non-Chinese people seized control of the Yellow River Valley in the 4th century and the Chinese court had to retreat to the south, Zu Di swore to recover this lost territory. One of his friends, also a general, once said, "I sleep with my weapon awaiting the dawn. My ambition is to kill the barbarian enemy, but I am always afraid that Zu will crack the whip before me." Thus, the reference means to try hard and compete to be first.

[50] See note 2.

40

I lean on the railing and lift my head to look
    at the cloudy sky.
All the mountains and rivers are dark.
Eastern Mongolia is lost and the date of her
    return is uncertain.[46]
The recovery of the Central Plains[47] depends
    on the youth.
Only the tongue of Changshan[48] can slay the
    villainous.
To kill the bandit we must wave the whip of
    Zu Di.[49]
I am ashamed to be curled up like a worm
    on Island.[50]
I grieve for my native land but what else can
    I say?

41

I have ten-thousand hopes that the
    revolutionary armies will complete their
    victory,
And help make the mining enterprises
    successful in the ancestral land.
They will build many battleships and come to
    the U.S. territory,
Vowing never to stop till the white men are
    completely annihilated.

40

憑欄翹首望雲天，
一片山河盡黯然。
東蒙失陷歸無日，
中原恢復賴青年。
誅奸惟有常山舌，
殺賊須揚祖逖鞭。
憶我埃崙如蜷伏，
傷心故國復何言。

41

萬望革軍成功竣，
維持祖國礦務通。
造多戰艦來美境，
滅盡白人誓不休。

42

The dragon out of water is humiliated by
    ants;
The fierce tiger who is caged is baited by a
    child.
As long as I am imprisoned, how can I dare
    strive for supremacy?
An advantageous position for revenge will
    surely come one day.

43

I left the village well behind me, bade
    farewell to my father and mother.
Now I gaze at distant clouds and mountains,
    tears forming like pearls.
The wandering son longed to be wealthy like
    Taozhu.[51]
Who would have known I would be
    imprisoned on Island?[52]
I beat my breast when I think of China and
    cry bitterly like Ruan Ji.[53]
Our country's wealth is being drained by
    foreigners, causing us to suffer national
    humiliations.
My fellow countrymen, have foresight, plan
    to be resolute,
And vow to conquer the U.S. and avenge
    previous wrongs!

44

If the land of the Flowery Flag[54] is occupied by
    us in turn,
The wooden building will be left for the
    angel's revenge.

[51] See note 12.

[52] See note 2.

[53] See note 31.

[54] See note 9.

92

42

蛟龍失水螻蟻欺，
猛虎遭囚小兒戲。
被困安敢與爭雄，
得勢復仇定有期。

43

拋離鄉井別椿萱，
遠盼雲山淚盈珠。
遊子志欲陶朱富，
誰知被圍埃崙間？

椎[1]膚中華囊阮籍，
利權外溢國恥兼。
同胞知機圖奮志，
誓奪美國報前仇。

1 原作"撫"

44

花旗旗其轉吾人佔[1]據，
木樓樓留與天使還仇。

1 原作"占"

45

If you have but one breath left, do not be
    discouraged from your purpose.
I respectfully exhort my brothers who are all
    talents of Chu.[55]
Having a sense of shame, one can eradicate
    shame.
Only by wielding the lance can one avoid
    certain defeat.
Do not say that we have not the means to
    level the ugly barbarians.[56]
I am searching for a method that will turn
    destiny back.
One-hundred-thousand men sharpen their
    swords,
Swearing to behead the Loulan[57] and open
    the grasslands and fallow fields.

46

The low building with three beams merely
    shelters the body.
It is unbearable to relate the stories
    accumulated on the Island[58] slopes.
Wait till the day I become successful and
    fulfill my wish!
I will not speak of love when I level the
    immigration station![59, 60]

By One From Taishan[61]

[55] During the Spring and Autumn Period (770 -476 B.C.), it is said that raw materials were produced in the state of Chu but were used by the state of Jin, meaning that native talent was used in a foreign land.

[56] The phrase, "Choulu," actually means enemy captives.

[57] During the Western Han dynasty (206 B.C. - 24 A.D.), Loulan was a state in the present Xinjiang province. Its king was simultaneously a vassal to the Han emperor and the Xiongnu "shanyu." In 77 B.C., the Han emperor ordered the assassination of the Loulan king, who had exhibited an unfriendly attitude toward the Chinese. Thereafter, Loulan came under Han rule.

[58] See note 2.

[59] Literally, customs station. This name for the immigration station may have been a carryover from the 19th century when Chinese entries and departures were processed at the San Francisco Customs House.

[60] The first character of each line forms a sentence, "Island awaits leveling."

[61] See note 14.

45

尚存一息志無灰，
敬勖同堂眾楚材。
知恥便能將恥雪，
揮戈方可免必裁。
莫道無謀芟醜虜，
思求有術把天回。
男兒十萬橫磨劍，
誓斬樓蘭闢草萊。

46

埃屋三椽聊保身，
崙麓積愫不堪陳。
待得飛騰順遂日，
劃除關稅不論仁。

台題

95

THE WEAK
SHALL CONQUER

The Japanese were detained too, but when they retaliated and started examining the Americans on Japanese ships for liver flukes, the two countries compromised. So when the Japanese arrived in the harbor, right away they were landed. Whereas, we citizens of China were deported and not allowed to enter. Isn't that a result of your own country's weakness?"

Mr. Yip, age 26 in 1921

There were quite a few Japanese there. They lived by themselves on one side and ate together at their own table. After only two days, they would leave for the city. Japan was a strong country then."

Mrs. Jew, age 19 in 1924

There were some Japanese and Korean women, but they lived in another room. They were locked up too, but they came and went in three days. Maybe that was because the Chinese were the ones who had faulty papers."

Mrs. Chan, age 23 in 1939

When I was there, we were treated very poorly. For example, other people, such as the Italians and Japanese, were provided with toilet paper and soap; just the Chinese didn't have it. We had to have it sent down to us from San Francisco. Because I had been there for six months, I was elected President of the Self-Governing Organization. We thought this was not very fair, so with some other officers of the Organization, I went and successfully negotiated for toilet paper and soap."

Mr. Tong, age 20 in 1932

The Japanese detained there were usually children born here and taken to Japan for their education. They had undoubtedly gone out of the country with affidavits bearing their photographs and they would present them on their way back. It was a matter of making sure it was the same child who had gone out. For that reason, they would have a shorter detention period. Other Japanese were temporary visitors and government officials, and maybe people in transit."

Immigration inspector #1, 1929-1940

China was a weak country in those days and because we were of the yellow race, we were considered inferior. We were uneducated, so in some respects, we couldn't blame the whites for looking down on us. We were coming in under false pretenses, so we were really asking for it. But that was the only way we could come over to find a better life."

Mr. Wong, age 12 in 1933

The Japanese detention quarters were next to ours. When they came to the United States, they all brought along their baggage and families. They did not need to have hearings and were free to go ashore within 24 hours. That could be because the diplomacy of a strong nation forced the lenient implementation of the immigration laws."

Mr. Ma, age 17 in 1922

ABOUT WESTERNERS

poems 47-56

折磨時日

47

I am distressed that we Chinese are detained
    in this wooden building.
It is actually racial barriers which cause
    difficulties on Yingtai Island.[62]
Even while they are tyrannical, they still
    claim to be humanitarian.
I should regret my taking the risks of coming
    in the first place.

[62] An island in the Nan Hai (Southern Lake), west of the Forbidden City in Peking. Emperor Guangxu (1875 - 1908) was imprisoned here by the Empress Dowager Cixi in 1898 after a coup d'etat to halt his reform programs.

48

I thoroughly hate the barbarians because they
    do not respect justice.
They continually promulgate harsh laws to
    show off their prowess.
They oppress the overseas Chinese and also
    violate treaties.
They examine for hookworms[63] and practice
    hundreds of despotic acts.

[63] Applicants for entry were examined for hookworm. During the earlier years, infestation with the parasite was cause for deportation. Later, patients were required to undergo medical treatment before landing.

49

I cannot bear to describe the harsh treatment
    by the doctors.
Being stabbed for blood samples and
    examined for hookworms[64] was even more
    pitiful.
After taking the medicine, I also drank
    liquid,[65]
Like a dumb person eating the *huanglian*.[66]

[64] See note 63.

[65] Liquid medicine.

[66] "Coptis teeta," a bitter herb. "A dumb person eating the 'huanglian'" is a victim who cannot voice his complaints to anyone.

47

傷我華僑留木屋，
實因種界厄瀛臺。
摧殘尚說持人道，
應悔當初冒險來。

48

詳恨番奴不奉公，
頻施苛例逞英雄。
凌虐華僑兼背約，
百般專制驗勾蟲。

49

醫生苛待不堪言，
勾蟲剌血更心酸。
食了葯膏又食水，
猶如啞佬食黃連。

50

It is indeed pitiable the harsh treatment of
　　our fellow countrymen.
The doctor extracting blood caused us the
　　greatest anguish.
Our stomachs are full of grievances, but to
　　whom can we tell them?
We can but pace to and fro, scratch our
　　heads, and question the blue sky.

51

I hastened here for the sake of my stomach
　　and landed promptly in jail.
Imprisoned, I am melancholy; even when I
　　eat, my heart is troubled.
They treat us Chinese badly and feed us
　　yellowed greens.[67]
My weak physique cannot take it; I am truly
　　miserable.

52

The barbarian issued orders to change rooms.
Running up and down, my breath grew short.
It was like warfare, when people's minds are
　　bewildered.
The scene resembled a stampede set off by
　　beacon smoke.[68]

50

刻薄同胞實可憐，
醫生刺血最心酸。
寃情滿腹憑誰訴？
徘徊搔首問蒼天。

51

爲口奔馳馳到監，
困愁愁食亦心煩。
薄待華人黃菜餐，
弱質難當實爲難。

52

蠻夷發令把房遷，
上下奔馳氣絕然。
恰似干戈人心亂，
聲勢猶如走烽烟。

53

I have lingered here three days moving again
   and again.
It is difficult to compare this to the peacefulness
   at home.
Life need not be so demeaning.
Rushing about so much, smoke came out of
   my mouth.

54

[69] One of the dreams of ancient China alchemists was to discover the pill of immortality. In one experiment, cinnabar and other chemicals were heated in a crucible; hence, the term, "cinnabar crucible."

[70] See note 1.

[71] A giant, mythical bird: the roc. It is reputed to fly 10,000 "li." Thus, the journey of the "peng" indicates a promising future.

Half of my life has been spent running here
   and there searching for fame.
I ask myself when I will be satisfied.
All medicine was useless when I contracted a
   fever.
I did not see a doctor, but still I was afraid.
I think the gods in heaven surely protected
   me.
I did not need an alchemist's crucible[69] and the
   sickness subsided of itself.
From now on when I hear a storm brewing in
   the Milky Way,
I will gaze the distance of one-thousand *li*[70]
   and resolve to rise to the heights of the
   peng.[71]

53

駐足三天遷復遷，
難比家居咁安然。
人生何苦如斯賤，
馳得勞勞口吐烟。

54

半生逐逐為求名，
借問何時可愜情？
葯石無靈成痼疾，
岐黃未遇却心驚。
蒼天想必神能祐，
丹鼎無需病自平。
從此聞颷雲漢起，
行看萬里奮鵬程。

1 余本作"須"

55

[72] During the political turmoil in China at the end of the Western Jin dynasty (265 - 316 A.D.), two princesses fled to a distant region for safety and ended up marrying commoners in a village. They were often unhappy and longed for their old homes. Their fellow villagers then built a terrace which they could ascend to gaze in the direction of their home.

Shocking news, truly sad, reached my ears.
We mourn you. When will they wrap your
    corpse for return?
You cannot close your eyes.
Whom are you depending on to voice your
    complaints?
If you had foresight, you should have regretted
    coming here.
Now you will be forever sad and forever
    resentful.
Thinking of the village, one can only futilely
    face the Terrace for Gazing Homeward.[72]
Before you could fulfill your ambition, you
    were buried beneath clay and earth.
I know that even death could not destroy your
    ambition.

56

[73] See note 40.

The young children do not yet know worry.
Arriving at the Golden Mountain,[73] they were
    imprisoned in the wooden building.
Not understanding the sad and miserable
    situation before their eyes,
They must play all day like calves.

55

噩耗傳聞實可哀，
弔君何日裹尸回？
無能瞑目憑誰訴？
有識應知悔此來。
千古含愁千古恨，
思鄉空對望鄉臺。
未酬壯志埋坯土，
知爾雄心¹死不灰²。

1 余本作"志"
2 余本作"恢"

56

少年子弟未知愁，
來到金山困木樓。
不悟¹眼前悲苦境，
還要終日戲如牛。

1 粵海春秋作"晤"

107

ABOUT WESTERNERS

It was a beautiful island with beautiful scenery. Every time we ate, we had to go way down these stairs. Everything tasted good to me, because I never had those things before. It was just the way they confined you, like in a prison, that made us feel degraded. When the white man goes to China, he doesn't get that kind of treatment. He is treated like a king in China."

Mr. Wong, age 12 in 1933

When we first came, we went to the administration building for the physical examination. The doctor told us to take off everything. Really though, it was humiliating. The Chinese never expose themselves like that. They checked you and checked you. We never got used to that kind of thing—and in front of whites."

Mr. Lee, age 20 in 1930

On arrival, we were examined for hookworm. I remember being handed a plastic basin to eliminate into. Before I came to Angel Island, I knew of a friend who shared his feces with another immigrant who couldn't eliminate at the moment. It was the same feces, but do you know, one was found to have hookworm and the other didn't!"

Mr. Tong, age 17 in 1921

There were quite a few people with me at the hospital who had hookworm. Most people in China had it. It was so common. I was supposed to go to the hospital alone, but I refused, so my mother kept me company. Women and children stayed together in one room. There were eight or ten beds. Every morning, the nurse brought us medicine. The nurses knew a few phrases of Chinese: 'Fun gow la! Hek fan la!', such common phrases to call us to sleep or eat. They were nice to us, soft-spoken and polite."

Mrs. Jew, age 19 in 1924

When you were sick, you would tell the female guard. They sent you to the hospital and always gave you laxatives. It tasted awful. You returned in a few days usually."

Mrs. Chan, age 23 in 1939

The guards at the wooden building disliked the new Chinese arrivals intensely. Night rules were strict: lights were shut off at 9 p.m., noise was not allowed. The tight security exceeded those for a prisoner and talking about it now, I cannot help but sigh deeply."

Mr. Ma, age 19 in 1922

Guards often shouted at us as if we weren't human; perhaps it was because some detainees previously had quarreled with them."

Mr. Tong, age 20 in 1939

When you didn't feel like getting up to eat, they dragged you up and forced you to go eat or go to the hospital. The women guards were in their fifties and sixties. They were mean, but they never hit us. Sometimes they scolded you. Some were nice. There was Mrs. (Katharine) Maurer,[24] who was pretty old. She would bring me materials to sew or yarn for knitting. She came once or twice a week and gave us a lot of things, especially at Christmas."

Mrs. Chan, age 23 in 1939

[24] Katharine Maurer, deaconess at the Angel Island station.

That night when I first arrived, the Jesus mother[25] recognized me, probably because my husband gave her my picture. She said, 'Good friend, good friend, tomorrow they will ask questions.' The other detainees said I was lucky to know her and that because of that, I would probably be released soon. Some of them had been there for over a year."

Mrs. Woo, age 23 in 1940

[25] See note 24.

There was a missionary lady[26] who came over once a week. When we had our menstrual period, we Chinese then used a kind of coarse paper, not menstrual pads like we do today. If your supply ran out, you gave her some money and asked her to buy some for you. And if there was any money left, she returned the change. She didn't preach to us, just helped us get things."

Mrs. Fong, age 22 in 1922

[26] See note 24.

If the guard came in and called out a name and said '*sai gaai*,'[27] it meant that that person was freed to land. If an applicant was to be deported, the guard would make motions as if he were crying."

Mr. Lee, age 20 in 1930

[27] Probably a corruption of "Hou sai gaai," a colloquial term meaning "good fortune." At other times, guards apparently also shouted, "Seung ngon," or "go ashore."

At that time, a new arrival was held for a hearing before a Board of Special Inquiry, as we called it. That consisted of two inspectors, a stenographer, and an interpreter. The inspector, to whom the care was assigned, was handed the file with any related files of that person's family. It was up to him to review the old file and start questioning the applicant about his birth and family home and in the course of the questioning and testimony, it would develop the applicant was either very much in accord with the old files or that there were rather serious discrepancies between him and the other family members. It was the only means we had, although it wasn't a very good method, because in a way, the Immigration Service built up a way for them to be coached and learn their testimony to get by. We just worked on the theory that this was the law and we had to carry it out. I felt each was entitled to a fair deal and I tried to give it to him as best as I could. In a way, it (laws discriminating against the Chinese) did touch me, and when the Exclusion Law was repealed, I thought that was a good thing.

"I started as a stenographer under the Civil Service and was assigned to the record vault to search records for about six years. There were masses of records of people from foreign countries, especially China. When Chinese or Japanese people came from the Orient and were detained, a file was started for that person with a file number made up of his ship's number and the page and line of the ship's manifest on which he was carried. Suppose the ship came into New York with the newcomer Chinese. The New York office, then Ellis Island, would send out here for any records we might have on the person's relatives. My job would be to go through the San Francisco records and pick out the person's father, brother, or sister's files, bundle them up, and send them to New York. It was the same way with Boston, Philadelphia, Seattle, and Los Angeles. About 90% of our files were on the Chinese because we handled persons of Oriental descent.

"They (interrogation rooms) were bright, airy rooms. There would be the stenographer's desk and another desk or two. When the applicant was brought in, he would be given a seat where he could be at ease and talk as he wished and where the interpreter would communicate with him. Around 15 percent of the cases I handled were women. I don't remember any prostitutes, except one instance after World War II. There were many, many boys coming through—twelve, 14, 15 years old, a lot of them smart kids. They were very sure of themselves.

"The testimony was taken directly on the typewriter. He would be questioned about his birthday, his parents, his brothers and sisters, and about the village he lived in. That might be quite brief or it might drag out with some inspectors to forty or fifty pages of typed testimony. It took from one to three or four days for him and the witnesses altogether. There usually was a certain field to be covered, according to his claims and the old claims. Usually you would start with the immigrant himself and check his testimony against his relatives'. If the testimonies matched, we had to give them the benefit of the doubt. A minor discrepancy would not carry much weight. If it was something serious...I remember a case of a boy whose father was bringing him in. He said his mother was so-and-so, but his father said his mother was so-and-so. He wasn't landed.

"After the Board heard the testimony, they would be pretty much in accord as to what was right and what was not. Any disagreement would mean a denial for the person. If two voted to land him and one voted to deny him, the dissenting member could appeal the case. But if he didn't wish to appeal, the person was landed. If the testimony was in accord, the file would be sent to the detention quarters and the person ordered to land. If denied, the person was not notified until the testimony was all summarized, but he would be given that notice eventually. If the applicant wished to appeal, the copy of the testimony would be sent to the central office in Washington and the attorney handling the case would be given a copy from which he made his appeal. They (Washington) would probably make its decision based on the transcript alone. More than 75 percent passed the interrogation at Angel Island. There could have been indications of fraud in some of them, but nothing that would stand up in court to debar them. Of those that were denied here, there was always an appeal to Washington and probably only 5 percent of those denied were ever really deported. Some who were deported came back and tried again, and made it. They knew you knew they were here before. If we found they were using another name, they could be excluded. Those deported had photographs taken that were held here to be checked. I've known of families of four or five coming together. They would question one briefly, just to a certain point. Then they would call back the first one and just go a little bit further. So they couldn't get together and talk about what they had just said.

"The interpreters we had were pretty good on most of the dialects. They would use one interpreter with one applicant. Then when they had a witness, they would change interpreters. The inspector in charge had to rotate the interpreters so that the first interpreter would usually not be available when recalled for a second hearing with the same applicant. I one time asked one of our interpreters what percentage of cases were fraudulent. I asked if 90 percent were. He said probably. I was aware of it from the beginning. I remember one case I was very sorry about. The father had brought a boy in, although it really was a daughter that he had had. She later came and I forget how he brought it up that she was really his daughter, and she really was, but the boys that he had gotten paid for bringing in had spoiled things for her. She was deported, but she married a G.I. and later came back.

"There were few bribes offered. I know it did happen, but the cases were very rare. I don't think I ever had anything offered to me, but in a few cases, some of the others had. It was something that was hard to prove. I was aware that coaching papers were being sneaked in. They (the administration) tried to prevent it. I did hear of a capsule being put in a bowl of soup with a note inside. They got the capsule but nothing developed from it. I know the kitchen help used to give them a lot of help (*laughs*), but there was nothing we could do about it."

Immigration inspector #1, 1929-1940

Around about the 1890's, many, many Chinese began to return to this country and they claimed to be coming back as natives. As a matter of fact, it would have been humanly impossible for most of them to be citizens because there were not many Chinese women over here. Most of them were denied admittance by the Immigration Service and they took their cases to court on *habeas corpus* proceedings and were landed by court order as citizens of the United States. From time to time, the Chinese went back to China and claimed to have been married and established a family, at least on paper. About 90 per cent boys and 10 per cent girls (*laughs*). They would return on re-entry certificates. From time to time, they would bring in their alleged children. That was the basis of all our work on the Board of Special Inquiry, testing the right of these new applicants to enter and remain, because they were coming in as alleged or potential citizens, not as aliens.

"I was a lot more thorough than most inspectors. I gave them a pretty good examination, and that involved a lot of different angles. We started by getting the data on the applicant himself: his name, age, any other names, and physical description. Then we would ask him to describe his family: his father—his boyhood name, marriage name, and any other names he might have had, his age, and so forth. Then we would go down the line: how many brothers and sisters described in detail—names, age, sex, and so forth. Then we would have to go into the older generations: paternal grandparents; then how many uncles and aunts and they had to be described. Then the village: the district, how many houses it was composed of, how arranged, how many houses in each row, which way the village faced, what was the head and tail of the village. Then the next door neighbors. Then describe the house: how many rooms and describe them. What markets they went to. Find out about the father's trip: when he came home, how long was he home, did he go to any special places, and describe the trip from his village to Hong Kong. In describing the home, we had to get the details of the main things in it and how the family slept, what bedroom each occupied. Sometimes it would take three or four hours to examine each one.

"We usually examined the applicant first. If there was any chance of a misunderstanding, we would call back the applicant and alleged father or brothers and try to reconcile them if possible. I found it an impossibility to get the applicant to change his testimony. He had learned that and by God, he was going to stick by that testimony, right or wrong. Major discrepancies would be cause for deportation. For example, if an applicant said his village consisted of ten houses and five rows, two houses in each row, and the alleged father said 30 houses and ten rows, or if they gave entire different circumstances about a trip they supposedly made together to Hong Kong, or if the applicant said his father had three brothers and the father said one brother. It was a question of testing them on family history. I couldn't see how it could have been handled any other way in the absence of all documentary evidence.

When a person came in from a little village, who would know them? There was just one way of finding out if the family belonged together as it was claimed and that was by testing their knowledge of their relationship."

Immigration inspector #2, 1929-1961

I just came out of college, nothing in sight, and so I said, 'Well, I'm going to try.' I knew Miss Cameron,[28] who was respected by the immigration people. Of course, she took a chance writing me a letter of introduction and vouching for me, but then, she knew my family background. The main selection criteria at that time was one's competence in handling the different Chinese dialects.

"No one interpreter sat throughout the same case. Because they were afraid of collusion between the interpreters and the applicants, they assigned one case to two or three interpreters. One interpreter would translate for the father, another one for the son, and another one for the mother. And that extended a case to one day, two days, three days. It (the length) all depended on whether the case was complicated or not. See, sometimes there was a contradiction between the father and son's testimonies, then they may call the father back from San Francisco. And it depended also on the inspector, whether he was long-winded, drawn-out, and detailed. But then, there were some inspectors, who could, if they sensed something was wrong, get right on to it. They got through a case very fast.

Now, it took longer to take care of a double-header—a mother and son as newcomers, or triple header—three in the family. The father may already have had some sons over here, so the sons would serve as corroborating witnesses. Or sometimes a friend or fellow villager would be a witness. So you had to take testimonies from two or three persons representing the petitioner. If the only witness lived out of town, like in New York or Chicago, they took the testimony out of the New York office or the Chicago office. That's why it took a lot of time adjudicating these cases.

"They were all pretty young, because by the very nature of it, claiming to be sons and daughters of natives or merchants, you couldn't apply once you became 21. Now unless it was a wife of a merchant, she could be any age. But nobody's going to bring in an old woman (*laughs*). During the interrogation, some were very calm and nonchalant. You asked a question, they answered. Then there were some who were very nervous, so I generally told them to just be quiet, take their time answering, and that kind of calmed them down a little bit. Some were a little hot-headed, with a chip on the shoulder. 'Why should you ask me all these questions?' and so on. In general, I think it was remarkable that the applicants, kids and women, were rather stoical. They stood up well, I think, by and large.

"It was so tedious, such minute detail, that you were bound to trip. Let me give you a humorous situation. I think it was a case of a triple-header. A mother and two kids came in at the same time, and a question by the inspector was: 'Is there a dog in the house?' If you live in a house, you know whether there's a dog or not, especially if the dog is your pet. So the mother said, 'Yes, we have a dog.' And another son, 'Yes, we have a dog.' And the third son, 'No, no dog.' So they called in the mother again, and the son, and they both said, 'Yes, yes, we had a dog.' And the other son was called in again. 'Did you say that you have a dog in the house?' 'Oh, we had a dog, but we ate that dog before we left! No dog!' Well, this was true. By the time he left the house, there was no dog. So, otherwise, it would be a very serious discrepancy if you lived in the same household and two said there's a dog and the other one said no.

"The interpreter didn't count in the ruling. We just interpreted what the man said or what was asked. But we did render an opinion as to that person's dialect. Because if I said the son spoke in the Chungshan[29] dialect and another interpreter said the father spoke in the Toishan[30] dialect, immediately, the inspector would smell a rat. And then, of course, the inspector would also make a judgement as to family resemblance, and those went into the record. This was very important because the appeal was often based on the fact that there was a close resemblance.

"Some inspectors were very fair-minded and impartial, and I would say, good. Then there were some who were very technical, and who were very prejudiced, who had no love for the Chinese.

"What happened was that in many cases where they were not real sons but paper sons, they were so well coached that their testimonies jibed. Whereas in the legitimate cases, they hadn't gone to the trouble of making up coaching books and preparing for it. They were the ones that got the wrong answers, because they thought it was going to be cut and dry.

"I remember one case. One came on a birth certificate and landed. Another person came and claimed that he was born in this country but that his birth certificate had been stolen. He was denied admission, but Washington sustained his appeal on the grounds that he might be the true one. The first one that came may have really stolen his paper. Then a third one came claiming the same thing, that the first two were false. So it was brought up to District Court and he was also landed. The court proceeded on the standpoint that no matter how many were fraudulent, one person was true, and it had not been proven that this third person was not true. So there was a certain amount of fairness in all this.

"Surprisingly, I don't remember any breakdowns when detainees were told their case had been denied. But there was one case of suicide while I was there, over in the women's quarters. This woman was destined for Chicago. She brought in a real son and a ringer. It was clear in my mind that one of them was a ringer. So this woman, when told her case was denied, felt that the whole thing was washed up, that she might be deported back to China, a most terrible shame. So she sharpened her chopstick and stuck it in her brain through the ear. Died. And even before Washington had a chance to deliberate on the case, Immigration phoned Washington about the suicide. So promptly the word came, 'Land them.' So they landed the two sons.

"It didn't happen often because I lived in Berkeley, but I do remember a case or two of someone asking me to try and bribe the inspector, and I said, 'Oh, no, no, no.' Sometimes it was very awkward. You told them you don't want the money and they turn around and say, 'It's because you feel it's too little.' But we had to protect ourselves against accusations from applicants, and generally, the lawyers and *bao wai*, the broker who took care of the case. It was the broker who told them 'I have to give money to the inspector and the interpreter.' But actually, he pocketed the money and just hoped the case would get through. If it didn't, he told them it was because the money wasn't enough. Now, I remember a case that was right here in Oakland. I had the unhappy duty of informing her that her case was denied. She hatefully said, 'It's because we didn't give you enough money. If we had, we would have been landed.' So for my own protection, I didn't want to get too close with those inspectors. Pretty soon, they might suspect something was going on with you two guys. So I had rather stayed away from them.

"Actually, the present system is best. Why bring them over to this country, give them a hearing, and then deny them. Why go through all that heartache, expense, and everything. Predetermine the case in Hong Kong, which is the best."

Immigration interpreter, 1928[31]

[28] Donaldina Cameron, Chinatown missionary.
[29] Cantonese pronunciation for Zhongshan, a district in the Pearl River delta.
[30] Cantonese pronunciation of Taishan, one of the districts in Sze Yap.
[31] Interviewed in 1976.

I was the only boy in the men's dormitories. Nobody took care of me, so I soon became dirty and full of lice. After three months, I was called for interrogation. The inspector only asked me my father's name; then I was landed. The interpreter told me I was lucky, because the sight of lice crawling all over me caused the inspector to cut short questioning and enabled me to arrive in Chinatown in time 'to eat chicken thigh' [32] on Chinese New Year's Eve."

Mr. Gin, age 6 in 1915

[32] The dark meat of the drumstick is considered the most delectable part of the chicken by most Cantonese.

I was there for two weeks. I was interrogated only once for two hours. I was tired and made mistakes during the interrogation but somehow passed. Those who claimed seven or eight sons and five or six grandsons were suspected and interrogated harshly because if he got through, that meant 30 to 40 more later. If one claimed one wife and one son, it was much easier to pass."

Mr. Low, age 15 in 1919

When it was my turn to be interrogated, they first made me wait in a small room. After awhile, they called me in and started asking me this and that, this and that, until I had a headache. After three or four hours of this, they confined me to a downstairs room where I stayed overnight. The next day, they questioned me again. They very seldom question you one day only and allow you to return upstairs. One strange question they asked me was: 'What is your living room floor made of?' I replied, 'Brick.' They said, 'Okay. What is the floor under your bed made of?' So I thought if the living room floor was brick, then the bedroom must also be brick. So I said, 'Brick!' They typed the answer down and didn't say anything. The next day, they asked the same question and I replied, 'Brick' again. They said my father had said it was dirt. What happened was that the floor was dirt at first, but later, after my father left for America, I changed the floor myself to brick. Where I really went wrong was in answering the question about who gave me the passage money. My father had written that he would send the money home to my mother to give me so that's what I said. But what happened was my father didn't really have the money and another relative loaned the money to my mother. So although I was a real son, I failed the interrogation. My deepest impression of Angel Island now was the rudeness of the white interrogators. They kept saying, 'Come on, answer, answer.' They kept rushing me to answer until I couldn't remember the answers anymore. And it wasn't just the whites. The Chinese interpreters did too."

Mr. Leung, age 24 in 1936

During the interrogation, if the inspector pursued a point, the situation would become tense. They even asked me where the rice bin was kept. Can you imagine? If your father had said the left side and the son, the right side, that won't do. In our days, we didn't have electricity, just kerosene lamps. And you know, a kerosene lamp's a moveable object. So what was I supposed to say if they asked where was the lamp kept? My father might have said the middle of the table or the end of the table. I didn't know. I couldn't understand why they asked such questions. They asked about **everything and anything**. When I was serving as a witness for my brother, they asked me how far the *shameen*[33] was from the wharf. I said, 'Very close.' The next time I was interrogated, they asked me the same question and I replied the same, 'Very close.' They then said, 'Okay, come get your brother tomorrow.' They were trying to trap me. I was interrogated only once for several hours in one day. I knew that most people who were interrogated in the morning would be landed the next day. It was bad if no news came by then."

Mr. Poon, age 18 in 1927

[33] Cantonese pronunciation of Shamian, an island on the Pearl River at Guangzhou, where the United States Consulate used to be located.

116

Sometimes the interrogator would try to trip you, like I told him the village's altar of worship was on the east side of the village. At the next session, he said my papa said it was on the west side. But I still said east side, and they all laughed."

Mr. Wong, age 12 in 1933

I was interrogated one day for several hours. They asked me so much, I broke out in a sweat. Sometimes they would try to trip you: 'Your husband said such-and-such and now you say this?' But the answer was out already and it was too late to take it back, so I couldn't do anything about it. If they said you were wrong, then it was up to them whether to land you or not. Later, upon landing, I noticed a white man kept coming around to my husband's laundry and looking at me through the glass window. That was how they checked you out to make sure you didn't go elsewhere."

Mrs. Chin, age 19 in 1913

There were good and bad hearing officers, differing according to the person's temperament. As far as my hearing officer was concerned, he was reasonable. The interpreter was Chinese, and the smoothness of the proceedings could hardly be faulted."

Mr. Ma, age 17 in 1922

I was interrogated for three days. The questions they asked me were baffling. After a day or two of questioning, it was not surprising that people would give a wrong answer here and there. I made the mistake of saying I was married. At that time, if someone coming as a merchant's son was married in China, he could not enter. My wife and I were separated for 17 years. She came as a G.I. wife only after I had served during World War II."

Mr. Tong, age 20 in 1932

I waited three weeks before I was interrogated. I was questioned three times and asked my name, village, population of the village, number of houses in the village lane, the neighbors living up and down the lane and their occupations. After each question, the interrogator would stop for a long time and look at my expression before continuing. It took more than an hour for each interrogation. The inspector's attitude was non-threatening and pleasant, but I felt frightened and threatened anyway, having listened to people who returned to the village tell of interrogations."

Mr. Low, age 25 in 1922

When it was time for the interrogation, they pointed out the room number and said it in Chinese. You would go, and when you reached a certain point, someone would direct you.

It was a Sam Yup[34] person who interpreted for me. He was very nice. There were very few questions, just for procedure's sake, like which direction did your house in China face, how many windows, who were your neighbors next door. I told him outright; after all, I did live there and was familiar with the place. Everything was true in my case, the surname, the name. If I couldn't remember, I just said it was about like that. The white immigration interrogator later told my husband he had a smart wife. My son was not interrogated, probably because he looked like my husband. It took almost an hour. They would ask questions and also make small talk."

Mrs. Woo, age 23 in 1940

[34]Three districts in the suburbs of Guangzhou: Nanhai, Panyu, Shunde.

Prior to interrogation, you were not allowed to have any visitors. The guards said, 'Here they come, here they come!' but they never let you see them. When I went, the interrogators were very thoughtful. The white lady gave me some candy and by the time I had finished eating my candy, the interrogation was over. It took not more than ten minutes. They asked a few questions, nothing much: what is your father's name, what village are you from, how old are you, so forth. Maybe they asked less questions than usual because they had questioned my husband first. They questioned him, then me, then my son. After they finished the interrogation, two days later, I was able to get on the ship. I took the boat and my relatives met me in San Francisco."

Mrs. Jew, age 33 in 1922

After two weeks, I was called in for interrogation. I waited a long while downstairs before it was my turn. You know how these government employees are. They would rather chat inside and take their time instead of working. I felt it didn't do any good to be afraid then. If they didn't believe you, all they could do was send you back. They couldn't beat you, so your heart could be at rest. At worst, I could say I sat there for two months and had free meals to boot."

Mr. Ng, age 15 in 1931

If things checked out in Hong Kong, I think they should have just let us land instead of making us suffer at Angel Island. If we failed the interrogation here, we would have then suffered twenty days aboard ship, seasickness, and all for nothing. In my case, I had to endure twenty months of prison-like confinement. Think how sad it all was."

Mrs. Chan, age 23 in 1939

118

When we first moved over there, my youngest girl was seven years old. One Saturday morning my girls got up and came into the bedroom and said that a man had just went through our back yard and up the hill. In due time they found the remains of a Chinese man in the water close to the island. He was trying to escape, but where to I don't know, because he couldn't get off the island. So whether he fell over one of the cliffs or what, I don't know. I would say that was about 1922. When they took a count, there was one missing. Of course, they searched the island and couldn't find anyone. Within a week, they found the body...in the Bay."

**Wife to a maintenance man
on Angel Island, 1920-1940**

DEPORTEES, TRANSIENTS

poems 57-69

寄
治
偉
里

[74]See note 30.

[75]The posthumous title of Han Yu (768 - 824 A.D.), scholar and official during the Tang dynasty (618 - 907 A.D.). In 819 he came under disfavor when he memorialized the throne against the elaborate ceremonies planned to welcome an alleged bone of Buddha. For this, he was exiled to Chaozhou in Guangdong province, then still an undeveloped region of jungles and swamps. On his way south, he bade farewell to his grandnephew at a snowy mountain pass, Lan Guan, in Shenxi, and composed a poem to express his feeling.

[76]March 13, 1917.

57

On a long voyage I travelled across the sea.
Feeding on wind and sleeping on dew, I tasted
    hardships.
Even though Su Wu was detained among the
    barbarians, he would one day return home.[74]
When he encountered a snow storm, Wengong
    sighed, thinking of bygone years.[75]
In days of old, heroes underwent many
    ordeals.
I am, in the end, a man whose goal is
    unfulfilled.
Let this be an expression of the torment which
    fills my belly.
Leave this as a memento to encourage fellow
    souls.

13th Day of the 3rd Month in the 6th Year of the Republic[76]

58

May I advise you not to sneak across the
    barrier.
Green waters surround a green hill on four
    sides.
Ascending to a high place, one does not see
    the shore.
To cross the green waters is the most difficult
    of difficulties.

Life is worth worrying about and you should
    restrain yourselves.
Do not treat these words as idle words.
Why not let them deport you back to China?
You will find some work and endure to earn
    a couple of meals.

57

梯航遠涉歷重洋，
風餐露宿¹苦自嘗。
蘇武淪胡歸有日，
文公遇雪嘆當年。
自古英雄多磨折²，
到底男兒志未伸。
滿腹苦衷聊代表，
留爲紀念勵同魂。

中華民國六年
三月十三日

1 原作 "宿露"
2 原作 "攝"

58

勸君切勿來偷關，
四圍綠水繞青山。
登高遠望無涯岸，
欲渡綠水難上難。

生命堪虞君自重，
斯言不是作爲閒。
盍任撥回歸國去？
覓些¹營生捱兩²餐。

1 余本作 "此"
2 余本作 "二"

123

77 When Han Xin (? - 196 B.C.) was a poor youth, a local bully tried to humiliate him by ordering him to crawl between his legs. Han obediently complied and became a laughing stock. later, Han Xin rose to become an important general serving the first emperor of the Han dynasty (206 -157 B.C.) and was made a marquis.

78 Goujian was king of the state of Yue (in the present province of Zhejiang). In 494 B.C. he was ignominiously defeated by King Fucha's armies from the state of Wu. Two decades later in 473 B.C., Yue recovered and returned to defeat Wu, whose territory was annexed to Goujian's domains. During Yue's recovery period, it was alleged that King Goujian slept on firewood and tasted gall bladder in order not to forget the bitterness and humiliation of his defeat. Fan Li (Taozhugong) was one of his important ministers during this period (see note 12).

79 See note 20.

80 Also known as Lu Shang or Taigongwang, Jiang was an important minister serving King Wen and King Wu of Zhou. According to a legend, his talents were not recognized until he was 70, when King Wen found him fishing on the Wei River. The king had him tutor his son, who later became King Wu. After helping King Wu conquer the Shang state, Jiang was made the marquis of Qi (in the present Shandong province).

59

I leave word for my compatriots not to worry
   too much.
They mistreat us but we need not grieve.
Han Xin was straddled by a bully's trousers
   yet became a general.[77]
Goujian endured humiliation and ultimately
   avenged his wrong.[78]
King Wen was imprisoned at Youli and yet
   destroyed King Zhou.[79]
Even though fate was perverse to Jiang
   Taigong, still he was appointed marquis.[80]
Since days of old, such has been the fate of
   heroes.
With extreme misfortune comes the
   composure to await an opportunity for
   revenge.

60

This is a message to those who live here not
   to worry excessively.
Instead, you must cast your idle worries to
   the flowing stream.
Experiencing a little ordeal is not hardship.
Napoleon was once a prisoner on an island.

59

寄語同胞勿過憂，
苟待吾儕毋庸愁。
韓信受袴為大將，
勾踐忍辱終報仇。
文王囚羑而滅紂，
姜公運斗亦封侯。
自古英雄多如是，
否極泰來待復仇。

60

寄語同居勿過憂，
且把閒愁付水流。
小受折磨非是苦，
破崙¹曾被島中囚。

１余本作"埃崙"

125

[81] At the end of the Qin dynasty in the 3rd century B.C., Xiang Yu (232 - 202 B.C.) led 8,000 young stalwarts from the region east of the Yangzi River (in the present province of Jiangsu) to vie for China's rule. He was, however, ultimately defeated by Liu Bang, who subsequently became the first emperor of the Han dynasty (206 - 195 B.C.). After losing nearly all his men, Xiang Yu chose to commit suicide rather than return to face the elders of his native region in defeat.

[82] See note 9.

[83] Lusong refers to Mexico. Chinese first came into contact with the Spanish in large numbers on the island of Luzon in the Philippines. Possibly because of the close connection of Mexico, another Spanish-speaking region, with the Manila trade, the latter became known as Da Lusong (Big Luzon) while the Philippines became Xiao Lusong (Little Luzon). During the exclusion era, many Chinese illegally entered the United States from Mexico.

[84] See note 31.

[85] Li Ling (? - 74 B.C.), a Han general, led an army of foot soldiers against the Xiongnu. After fighting against great odds, he was forced to surrender. The Han emperor subsequently executed his mother, younger brother, wife, and children. Li Ling was a contemporary of Su Wu (see note 30) and the grandson of Li Guang (? - 119 B.C.), another famous general who fought the Xiongnu.

61

Barred from landing, I really am to be pitied.
My heart trembles at being deported back to
    China.
I cannot face the elders east of the river.[81]
I came to seek wealth but instead reaped
    poverty.

62

I entered the land of the Flowery Flag[82] by
    way of Lusong.[83]
Conditions at the border were strict and I
    was not clever.
In the wooden jail, I was imprisoned for
    days.
Now I am to be deported back in the steel
    vessel, *Persia*.

When Ruan Ji reached the end of the road,
    who took pity on his weeping?[84]
In a distant land, Li Ling sadly sighed in
    vain.[85]
There is nothing that can be done about
    misfortune caused by tyranny.
Fate is unlucky and times are perverse;
    therefore, I suffer these ordeals.

61

阻攔上埠實堪憐，
撥回祖國也心驚。
無面見江東父老，
只望求富反求貧。

62

假道呂宋走花旗，
關情嚴密不知機。
監牢木屋囚困日，
波斯鐵船被撥期。

窮途阮籍誰憐哭？
絕域李陵空嘆愁。
無可奈何事制厄，
命蹇時乖受此磨。

63

[86] More commonly "Lim," "Lam," or "Lum" in the United States.

[87] Shiqi. See note 42.

Lin,[86] upon arriving in America,
Was arrested, put in a wooden building,
And made a prisoner.
I was here for one autumn.
The Americans did not allow me to land.
I was ordered to be deported.
When the news was told,
I was frightened and troubled about returning
    to my country.
We Chinese of a weak nation
Can only sigh at the lack of freedom.

Written by a Taoist From the Town of Iron[87]

64

Crude Poem Inspired by the Landscape

[88] i.e., mail service.

[89] See note 29.

The ocean encircles a lone peak.
Rough terrain surrounds this prison.
There are few birds flying over the cold hills.
The wild goose messenger[88] cannot find its
    way.
I have been detained and obstacles have been
    put my way for half a year.
Melancholy and hate gather on my face.
Now that I must return to my country,
I have toiled like the *jingwei* bird in vain.[89]

63

林到美洲，
逮[1]入木樓。
成爲囚犯，
來此一秋。
美人不准，
批撥回頭。
消息報告，
回國驚憂。
國弱華人，
嘆不自由。

　　鐵城道人題

1 原作"隸"

64

感景拙詠

滄海圍孤峯，
崎嶇困牢籠。
鳥疎寒山緻，
鴻使莫尋踪。
留難經半載，
愁恨積滿容。
今將歸國去，
空勞精衛功。

65

[90]The poet here uses the poetic name of Xiangjiang ("Fragrant River") rather than the conventional Xianggang ("Fragrant Harbor").

Bidding farewell to the wooden building, I
   return to Hong Kong.[90]
From hence forward, I will arouse my
   country and flaunt my aspirations.
I'll tell my compatriots to inform their fellow
   villagers.
If they posess even a small surplus of food
   and clothing,
They should not drift across the ocean.

66

[91]i.e., he had made no progress.

[92]Southeast Asia.

For one month I was imprisoned; my slippers
   never moved forward.[91]
I came on the *Manchuria* and will return on
   the *Mongolia*.
But if I could make the trip to Nanyang,[92] I
   would.
Why should America be the only place to
   seek a living.

65

木樓永別返香江，
從此興邦志氣揚。
告我同胞談梓里，
稍餘衣食莫飄洋。

66

乙月被囚履不前，
滿州輪來蒙古旋。
但得南洋登程日，
求活何須美利堅？

67

I abandoned my native village to earn a
    living.
I endured all the wind and frost to seek fame.
I passed this land to get to Cuba.[93]
Who was to know they would dispatch me to
    a prison on a mountain?

68

People from Doumen[94] are going to Daxidi,[95]
Having been in the wooden building for
    more than ten days.
From Daxidi, there are people returning to
    the Mountains of Tang.[96]
How were they to know this would be such a
    callous city?
There are people returning and there are
    people leaving.
Having wasted over three-hundred silver
    dollars,
If I do not get to this city, I will be unhappy.
If I return home, my parents would be
    extremely grief-torn.
Unpaid interest would be piled one on top of
    another,
Not knowing when it would be repaid to the
    lender.

[93] Angel Island was also used as a detention facility for transients to and from Cuba, Mexico, and other Latin American countries. In 1921 the Mexican government banned the immigration of Chinese labor into Mexico.

[94] An area in the southwest of the Pearl River Delta, Doumen was formerly part of the Zhongshan district. Today, it forms a separate district.

[95] Tahiti? Identification of place is uncertain.

[96] See note 37.

67

拋離家鄉作營謀，
風霜捱盡爲名求。
路經此地來古巴，
誰知撥我入山囚？

68

斗門人往大溪地，
來到木屋十日餘。
溪地有人回唐山，
誰知此埠極難爲。
有人回來有人去，
使枉洋銀三百餘。
不到此埠心不忿，
回家父母苦極悲。
留下利息重重疊，
未知何日還他主？

1 原作 "至"
2 原作 "汪"

[97] See note 93.

[98] A contraction of "the whip of Zu Di." (See note 49).

69

Detained in this wooden house for several
    tens of days,
It is all because of the Mexican exclusion
    law[97] which implicates me.
It's a pity heroes have no way of exercising
    their prowess.
I can only await the word so that I can snap
    Zu's whip.[98]

From now on, I am departing far from this
    building.
All of my fellow villagers are rejoicing with
    me.
Don't say that everything within is Western
    styled.
Even if it is built of jade, it has turned into a
    cage.

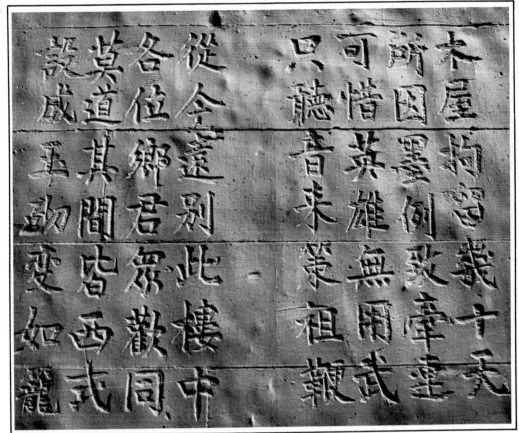

大廈拘習載十夫
所因墨例致牽連
可惜英雄無用武
只聽音未策祖鞭
從今遠別此樓中
各位鄉君眾歡同
莫道其間皆西武
設成玉勁變如麗

DEPORTEES, TRANSIENTS

I didn't really want to come, but my father bought me a paper. I figured I'd come and stay for three months or so and go back. My father and three uncles were already here in the United States. The man who claimed me as his son came from Mexico. There were some contradictions in our testimonies, so we hired an attorney. It was no use. They deported me, along with the old-timers who had gone back home and come back but were found to be infected with hookworm. I left my home on the sixth day of the sixth moon and I returned on the sixth day of the sixth moon the following year. It was exactly one year.

"There was a lot of writing on the walls. It must have been done by people who liked to write. After borrowing money to come here and then being locked in and unable to land, naturally you were frustrated. You start thinking and you write something. What a bother coming here. You weren't born rich. You didn't come here with money, just with a piece of paper."

Mr. Yip, age 26 in 1921

The people at Angel Island wrote poems all over the walls, wherever the hand could reach, even in the bathroom. Some were carved, but most were written with ink. There were many carved in the hall leading to the basketball court, because the wood there was softer. It was not easy finding space on the wall to compose a poem, so sometimes when I thought of something lying in bed, I would bend over and write a poem under my bed, which was made of canvas. Sometimes, when someone didn't like what another person wrote, he would deface the poem, saying, 'What a smart aleck, trying to write poetry like the others.' Sometimes, people fought over poems. A lot of people there didn't know how to write poetry. They weren't highly educated, but they knew some of the rules of poetry. You can't say the poems were great, but they expressed real feelings. They were works of the overseas Chinese and therefore part of the history of the overseas Chinese."

Mr. Ng, age 15 in 1931

It was like songs people would sing. It was very common. I didn't write on the walls, but I did compose some poems, crying at the same time."

Mrs. Chan, age 23 in 1939

Someone told me that one woman failed the interrogation and tried to drown herself; so the husband returned to China with her."

Mrs. Fong, age 22 in 1922

I thought the poems on the walls were ridiculous. Some of them exaggerated conditions there because the writers were ignorant people from the countryside. When I was allowed to land, I didn't want to leave; I was having such a good time."

Mr. Lee, age 21 in 1934

I n general, the feelings were: one, an eagerness to leave and go on to San Francisco, and two, to get the interrogation over with. Until then, no one was very happy. At the time, we did not understand America's immigration laws. We were told that we had to come through Angel Island. Most did not think to protest. If the food was bad, we put up with it. Our treatment wasn't cruel, so we just endured the period and hoped for it to pass. Only those who were detained and separated from relatives for a long time and who were going through the appeal process after spending a lot of money to come in the first place suffered. They were the ones who wrote the angry and bitter poems. But looking back now at how the United States treated Chinese and Asian immigrants, we can see how unequal and unfair the treatment was."

Mr. Dea, age 26 in 1939

S ome used ink brushes to write poems on the walls, usually the educated ones from back home. We younger men were too busy playing to pay them much attention. They would say they were from Toishan[35] or some other region, but they wouldn't divulge their names. The guards never entered the room, so they didn't know what was going on inside."

Mr. Quan, age 16 in 1913

[35]See note 8.

IMPRISONMENT IN THE WOODEN BUILDING

Poem published in the *Chinese World*, March 16, 1910

PREFACE

This manuscript was sent through the mail by a person detained in the wooden building on Angel Island. We shall print the manuscript unchanged for all to read. The writer has written a sad and angry essay based on his personal experience. Is it with blood? Tears? Ink? We know that when all our compatriots at home and abroad read it, they will be extremely provoked. However, even though our compatriots may be incensed, what good is it if we merely look at one another helplessly and weep like prisoners of Chu?[99] If we do not firmly resolve to stir ten-thousand multitudes as with one heart and plan to make the ancestral land wealthy and strong, to make the glory of our yellow dragon national flag[100] shine on both shores of the Pacific Ocean, then it will not be easy to wipe out this humiliation.

Commentary by the editor of the *Chinese World*

I have often thought of Su Wu, who gnawed on snow and dined on felt,
    yet maintained his loyalty to the Han dynasty;[101]
And of the king of Yue, who slept on firewood and tasted the gall bladder in
    order to take vengeance on the enemy state of Wu.[102]
The forefathers frequently met with misfortune;
Our elders experienced all forms of difficulties and hardships.
In the end, they achieved recognition in history
And exhibited their might to the barbarians.
By so doing, they quelled their anxiety
And also pacified their lifelong desire.
It is only we who have run into bad fortune.
The course of events in our lives have for the most part gone astray.
Drifting like grass to a foreign land, we are forever being forced into
    imprisonment as at Youli.[103]
As we depart from the native village, we shed tears again and again, as if we had
    reached the end of the road.[104]
When I arrived in America, all I could do was gaze at the sea water in vain.
The ship docked at the wharf and I was transferred to the lonely Island.[105]
Ten *li*[106] from the city, I set foot on a lonely peak.
The three-story wooden building is as solid as the Great Wall.
Jail room after room, the lock of the North Gate is secure for long periods.[107]
Together with several hundred countrymen, it is a slim hope to be the one fish
    to elude the net.
Half a thousand of the yellow race are here, feeling lost like birds in a fine, mesh
    net.
Sometimes, we look up and gaze,
The mutual playing of Tartar pipes adding to our disconsolate sorrow.
Or we tilt our ears to listen,
The plaintive neighing of herded horses doubling our listless thoughts.
In the daytime, we dine on buttermilk, following in Yan Hui's footsteps, a
    basket of rice and a gourd of water.[108]
At night, we cover ourselves with a single blanket, like the clothing of rushes
    worn by Min Qian.[109]
When we wash our hands and feet in the morning, it is all with salty tidewater.
Sometimes we drink liquid; it is never other than turbid water.[110]
In this newly opened wild land, the environment is not agreeable.
Drinking water, many developed coughs.
Sipping it, not so few developed sore throats.

A hundred symptoms of sickness developed; it is difficult to put our misery into words.

At times when someone happened to anger the barbarians, they would beat him with fists and feet.

If they felt a brutal impulse, they would aim a gun at us.

They counted the number of people like the Prince of Qin reviewing his troops.[111]

Although we are surrounded several laps by mounted troops, we still have the clever strategems of Han Xin.[112]

Brothers cannot pass one word to each other, separated far from one another as if by mountains and passes.

Even though friends and relatives wish to comfort our hearts, they are separated by a distance as great as heaven and earth.

Being here, I wish to cry out to heaven, but heaven does not hear.

Entering this room, I wish to call to the earth, but the earth does not answer.

The trees are also gloomy outside the prison; a hundred birds cry mournfully.

Clouds and mists enshroud the mountain-side; a thousand animals, startled, flee.

This is what is known as living with trees and stones and roaming with the deer and wild boars.

Alas! Alas!

The scenery evokes my emotions.

Everywhere is desolation.

Grief and suffering has sent me here.

Why is life so?

There were those who were more miserable, whose pulses were taken several times; although well, they might just as well have been sick.

Their private parts were examined several times; and although their bodies were wrapped, it was as if they were naked.

May I ask the Quanrong,[113] "Why are you subjecting us to such extremes?"

Alas, for our kind, there is no recourse.

Even if we scraped the surface of all the bamboo on the Zhongnan Mountains, we could not write all our words of discontent.[114]

If we used all the waves of the Eastern Sea, we could not wash clean our appearance of shame.

Some say that when Emperor Min of Jin served wine at the barbarian's court, he did not decline the shame of wearing blue clothes.[115]

After the Han army surrendered to the barbarians, Li Ling once beat his breast and poured out his grievances.[116]

Now if even the people of old were like this, could it be people of today are the only ones who cannot bear it?

Moreover, when events are hard pressed and the situation desperate, what else
is there to say?
To conceal weapons and bide our time would only be indulging in useless
fantasy.
Alas, yellow souls suffer under the brute force of the white race!
Like shouting at a dog which has lost its home, we are forced into jail.
Like a pig chased into a basket, we are sternly locked in.
Our souls languish in a snowy vault; we are really not even the equal of cattle
and horses.
Our tears shower the icy day; we are not even equal to bird or fowl.
But since I came to this corner of the ocean, my temperament enjoys the
reading of newspapers.
They say that my old village and native land is laid open like a pea pod and
divided like a melon.
I grieve for an entire civilized nation swallowed up by wolves and bitten by
tigers.
(Parts deleted in original, published version)
I am about to see four-hundred million Chinese people again become slaves to
several nations;
Five-thousand years of history endangered and destroyed like India.[117]
It is indeed regrettable.
How can I refrain from speaking out?

[99]i.e., a held prisoner; a person in difficult straits.

[100]The flag of China under the imperial Qing government.

[101]See note 30.

[102]See note 78.

[103]See note 20.

[104]See note 31.

[105]See note 2.

[106]See note 1.

[107]i.e., a guarded door.

[108]Yan Hui (521-490 B.C.), the poorest of Confucius' disciples, ate very simply and yet was content.

[109]Min Ziqian (536-487 B.C.) or Min Sun, a disciple of Confucius, was treated cruelly by his stepmother when he was young. She used to clothe him in rushes, which did not keep out the winter cold.

[110]At the time, the immigration station did not have any fresh water tanks. Drinking water came from a spring, which at one point, contained traces of fecal contamination (Letter from L.C. Steward, acting commissioner, to the Commissioner-General of Immigration, December 19, 1910).

[111]The title of Li Shimin before he became the second emperor of the Tang dynasty (627-649 A.D.). He was a general prior to becoming emperor.

[112]See note 77.

[113]Barbarians living west of the Chinese states during the Zhou dynasty (1122 B.C.-249 B.C.).

[114]See note 21.

[115]In 316 A.D., during a chaotic period when a number of non-Chinese people were fighting for domination of northern China, Emperor Min of the Jin dynasty (313-316 A.D.) was captured by the Xiongnu and forced to perform such humiliating acts as serving wine to the victors.

[116]See note 85.

[117]During this period when China was threatened by the great powers, Chinese patriots often used India, which was then ruled by the British, as an example to alert their countrymen against the threat of foreign aggression to China's sovereignty.

此稿由被囚烟租埃崙木屋中人寄來。亟照
原稿登錄，以供眾覽。筆者以身受之苦，作悲
憤之文。血耶？淚耶？墨耶？吾知海內外同胞
讀之，必生無限激刺矣。雖然，吾同胞雖有無
限之激刺，空作楚囚之對泣，亦何濟於事。若
非發奮振作，萬眾一心，以共圖祖國之富強，
使我黃龍國旗，輝映於太平洋兩岸，未易一雪
此恥耳。

記者誌
（原刊三藩市世界日報，
一九一〇年三月十六日）

木屋拘囚序

嘗思嚙雪餐氈，蘇武守漢朝之節；

臥薪嘗胆，越王報吳國之讎。

古人坎坷屢遇，

前輩艱辛備嘗。

卒克著名於史册，

振威於蠻夷，

以解衷懷之憂，

而慰畢生之願也。

獨我等時運不濟[1]，

命途多舛。

蓬飄外國，永遭羑里之囚；

離別故鄉，頻灑窮途之淚。

躬到美域，徒觀海水之汪洋；

船泊碼頭，轉撥埃崙之孤島。

離埠十里，托足孤峯。

三層木屋，堅如萬里長城；

幾度監牢，長扃北門鎖鑰。

143

同胞數百，難期漏網之魚；
黃種半千，恍若密羅之雀。
有時舉頭而眺，
胡笳互動，益增惆悵之悲；
或者傾耳而聽，
牧馬悲鳴，倍覺無聊之想。
日餐醬酪，步顏子之簞瓢；
夜蓋單氈，同閔騫之蘆服。
朝則盥濯，盡是鹹潮；
時而飲滋，無非濁水。
矧遘荒新闉，水土欠和
飲焉而咳嗽者甚繁，
啜焉而喉痛者不少。
病端百出，苦楚難云。
間有偶觸胡怒，拳脚交加。
忽起狼心，彈炸向指。
人數目算，秦王之點兵尚存；
戎馬重圍，韓信之妙計猶在。

兄弟莫通一語，遠隔關山；

親朋欲慰寸衷，相離天壤。

處此間也，欲籲天而天無聞；

入此室也，欲叫地而地不應。

且也樹木陰翳於囚外，百鳥悲啼；

雲霞垂覆於山前，千獸駭走。

正所謂與木石居，與鹿豕遊者矣。

嗟！嗟！

觸景生情，

荒涼滿目。

愁難遣此，

命也何如？

尤有慘者，診脈幾回，無病宛然有病；

驗陰數次，裹身一若裸身。

借問犬戎，夫何使我至極？

哀哉吾輩，然亦無如之何。

雖削南山之竹，寫不盡牢騷之詞；

竭東海之波，流不淨慚愧之狀。

或者曰，狄庭行酒，晉愍不辭青衣之羞；

漢軍降奴，李陵曾作椎心之訴。

古人尚如此，今人獨不忍乎？

夫事窮勢迫，亦復何言？

藏器待時，徒空想像。

嗚呼！白種強權，黃魂受慘。

叱喪家之狗，強入牢籠；

追入笠之豚，嚴加鎖鑰。

魂消雪窖，眞牛馬之不如；

淚灑冰天，洵禽鳥之不若也。

但我躬既竄海曲，性品悦看報章。

稱説舊鄉故土，荳剖瓜分；

哀憐舉國斯文，狼吞虎噬。

（中略）

將見四百兆之華民，重爲數國之奴隸；

五千年之歷史，化爲印度之危亡。

良可慨也，

尚忍言哉？

| 世界日報作 "齊"

APPENDIX
poems 1-66

1

People who enter this country
Come only because the family is poor.
Selling their fields and lands,
They wanted to come to the land of the Flowery Flag.[118]
The family all looks to you.
Who is to understand it is the most difficult of
    difficulties!

2

Living at home, there were no prospects for
    advancement.
The situation forced one to go to another country.
Separated from the clan, a thousand miles away,
Apart from the ancestors, we are no longer close to
    one another.

3

It was four days before the Chongyang Festival[119]
When I transferred to a ship in Hong Kong.
Everybody is still here.
Our feet have been bound here for almost half an
    autumn.

Written by one going to Mexico

4

My parents are old; my family is poor.
Cold weather comes; hot weather goes.
Heartless white devils,
Sadness and anger fill my heart.

1　入此國之人：
　　因爲家貧起。
　　賣田又賣地；
　　欲往來花旗。
　　家人向住你¹；
　　誰知難上難。
　¹ 舊金山週報作 "治"

2　居家無步進；
　　他邦勢逼趁。
　　離宗千里遠；
　　別祖不相近。

3　重陽少四日；
　　香港付輪舟。
　　大家仍在此；
　　繫足將半秋。

　　往墨僑題

4　親老家貧；
　　寒來暑往。
　　無情白鬼；
　　悲憤填膺。

150

5

Abandoning wife and child, I crossed an entire ocean.
   I do not know how much wind and frost I've
   weathered; it was because my family was poor
   that I searched for white jade.[120]
Bidding farewell to relatives and friends, I drifted
   10,000 *li*.[121] It is difficult to keep track of all the
   rain and snow I've endured; it is all due to a
   harsh purse with a reverence for copper coins.

5

拋妻子，重洋歷盡，不知受幾多風霜，

　　　祇爲家貧求白璧；

別親朋，萬里飄流，難計捱一切雨雪，

　　　都緣囊澀重青蚨。

6

Flocks of fellow villagers do not refrain from
   spending thousands of gold pieces to get
   to America.
Several hundred compatriots invested huge sums but
   are now imprisoned on Island.[122]

6

梓里成羣，千金不惜，圖走美；

同胞數百，巨資投擲，困埃崙。

7

The five-colored flag of China flies all over the globe;[123]
   the nations under heaven all lose heart.[124]
Ten-thousand armies punish the foreign lands; the
   states of Europe all tremble with fear.

7

五旗飄寰球，天下諸邦皆喪胆；

萬軍誅異蜮¹，歐洲各國盡寒心。

１原作"域"

8

Today, we brothers are imprisoned in a jail; it is only
   because of our ancestral land.
If our countrymen want freedom in the future, then they
   must make an effort.

8

今日兄弟困牢籠，祇爲祖國；

他日同胞欲自由，務須努力。

9

As a traveller in wind and dust, half the time it was
  difficult.
In one month, I crossed to the end of the ocean.
I told myself that going by this way would be easy.
Who was to know that I would be imprisoned at
  Devil's Pass?

10

When I left, my parents regretted it was so hurried.
The reason I tearfully swallow my resentment is
  because of poverty.
Wishing to escape permanent poverty, I fled overseas.
Who caused my destiny to be so perverse that I
  would become imprisoned?
The victim of aggression, people of our nation mourn
  the desperate times.
I feel sorely guilty for having not yet repaid my
  parents' kindness.
Grieving the cold night, the insects now make noise.
Not only do I sob silently, but my throat tastes bitter.

By Smiley Jann[125]

11

Imprisoned in this wooden building, I am always sad
  and bored.
I remember since I left my native village, it has been
  several full moons.
The family at home is leaning on the door, urgently
  looking for letters.
Whom can I count on to tell them I am well?

Prisoners in this wooden building constantly suffer
  sadness and boredom.
I remember the hardships I had to endure when I
  was coming here.
I cannot prophesy which day I will cross the
  barrier.[126]
The years and months are easily spent in vain.

Composed by an old man from Taishan[127]

9　風塵作客半時難；
　　涉盡重洋一月間。
　　自問假途容易事；
　　誰知就困鬼門關。

10　離時父母恨忽忽；
　　飲怨漣漣也爲窮。
　　欲免長貧奔海外；
　　誰教命舛困囚中？
　　侵凌國族悲時切；
　　未報親恩抱罪隆。
　　今也鳴蟲哀冷夜；
　　不單幽咽苦喉嚨。

11　困囚木屋常愁悶；
　　憶別家鄉月幾圓。
　　家人倚望音書切；
　　憑誰傳語報平安？

　　木屋監囚愁悶多；
　　記憶來時歷苦楚。
　　過關未卜是何日；
　　空令歲月易蹉跎。

台山氏翁題

12

I went east to Asia; I went west to Europe.
I came to the South, to North America, where the
harsh exclusion laws cause me worry.
Allowing you to enter the place of imprisonment,
Even if you don't shed tears, you will lower your
head.

13

Pacing back and forth, I leaned on the window sill and
gazed.
The revolving sun and moon waxed and waned,
changing again and again.
I think about my brothers a lot, but we cannot see one
another.
The deep, clear water casts reflections as waves toss in
sympathy.

14

The cool wind and bright moon makes for a pitiful night.
The desolate feeling is aggravated by my solitary body
under the quilt in the wooden building.
The traveller thinks of his native village, where he once
kept company with a willow.
You, my dear, had no intention of travelling because of
your fondness for the banana plant by the window.
Su'e[128] does not know the suffering among mankind.
The whites only imprison sojourners from Dongya.[129]
It is unlike living in the village, ploughing and studying.
A leisurely life with firewood and rice, one is content
using a basket and gourd.[130]

15

Each day my sorrow increases as I stay on Island.[131]
My face, as well, grows sallow and my body, thin.
My detention and mistreatment has not yet ended.
I am afraid my petition will be denied and I, sent back.

By Chen

12 東走亞兮西走歐；
　南來北美苛禁愁。
　任君入到囚困地；
　若不流涕也低頭。

13 徘徊瞻眺倚窗邊，
　日月盈昃轉改轉。
　孔懷兄弟難相望，
　淵澄取映浪拋憐。

14 風清月朗可憐宵；
　木屋孤衾倍寂寥。
　客有鄉思眠伴柳；
　卿無旅意戀窗蕉。
　素娥未曉人間苦；
　白種偏因東椏[1]僑。
　不若村居耕與讀；
　優悠柴米樂簞瓢。
1 中山縣村名，方本作 "東亞"

15 埃崙居處日添愁；
　面亦黃兮身亦瘦。
　留難[1]磋磨猶未了；
　最怕批消[2]打回頭。
　　　　　　　陳題
1 舊金山週報作 "留連"
2 舊金山週報作 "拋消"

153

16

Quietly keeping my feelings to myself, I feel depressed.
My colleagues and I together call helplessly to heaven.
When do we whip our horses to cross the pass at Tong
    Guan? [132]
Let me first wave the whip of Zu Di. [133]

17

I have been imprisoned on Island [134] for seven weeks.
In addition, I do not know when I can land.
It is only because the road of life has many twists and
    turns
That one experiences such bitterness and sorrow.

18

Even though it is said that drifting is a man's lot,
Why am I imprisoned without guilt of crime?
Giving repentance and regrets to heaven, I reprimand
    myself daily.
Ask the blue heaven if I do or not?

19

When I think about it, it is really miserable.
For what reason does the blue heaven today
Imprison this humble person in a wooden building?
With no trace of tidings, it is really distressing.

20

Since our parting, another autumn has yet arrived.
I have become a distant traveller of far away places.
Remembering your great kindness, I know in my heart I
    have not repaid you.
Hoping to send good tidings, I'll depend on writing
    letters.

16 默默含情意黯然；
吾儕同喚奈何天。
幾時策馬潼關渡；
許我先揚祖逖鞭。

17 埃崙被困七星期；
上岸何時也未知。
祇爲命運多曲塞；
繚受是中苦與愁。

18 漂泊雖云男兒事；
奈何無罪入囚途。
如天懺恨天天數；
問句蒼天知有無。

19 自己想來眞苦楚；
蒼天今日因如何，
困我鄙人在木樓？
音信無跡實難過。

20 握別依然又一秋；
天涯作客遠方遊。
回憶高情心未償；
望傳佳語藉書郵¹。

¹ 余本作 "賴"

154

21

I left my native village and drifted to the American
  continent.
The moon has waned and waxed in turn several times.
My family anxiously waits for me to mail them news.
It is difficult to meet the wild geese[135] and my sorrow is
  unending.

22

I remember since boarding a ship to America
Till now, the moon has waned twice.
I want to send a letter of comfort, but regret that there is
  little time.
The family is expectant, but their hopes are in vain.

23

I came to the United States because I was poor.
How was I to know fate would be so perverse as to
  imprison me?
News and letters do not reach me and I can only
  fantasize.
I hear no news, so who sympathizes with me?

24

I have been in the wooden building for more than ten
  days.
My eyes have seen people being deported back.
Witnessing that scene makes one sad.
Spending more than five-thousand golden coins,
I drifted alone to this place.
If I am unlucky enough to be deported, my parents will
  be grieved.
The interest piles one on top of another.
I do not know yet when it will be completely repaid to
  the creditor.

21　離鄉飄流到美洲；
　　月缺重圓數輪流。
　　家人切望音信寄；
　　鴻雁難逢恨悠悠。

22　憶自動輪來美洲；
　　迄今月缺兩輪流。
　　欲寄安書恨期乏；
　　家人懸望空悠悠。

23　我爲家貧來美境；
　　誰知命蹇困監牢。
　　音信莫達空思想；
　　消息無聞孰可憐。

24　來到木屋十日餘[1]；
　　眼見有人撥回去。
　　令人見景亦生悲；
　　耗費金錢[2]五千餘。
　　孤身飄流到此處；
　　不幸撥回父母悲。
　　嗰哋[3]利息重重疊；
　　未知何日還清主[4]。

1 余本作 "十餘日"
2 余本作 "刀"
3 余本作 "哥的"
4 余本作 "了"

25

The ship set sail last year in the sixth moon.
I did not expect to be in this prison now.
I squandered a thousand and several hundred.
All my life I have been wretched, helpless, and now it
    has implicated my elder brother.

26

I raise my brush to write a poem to tell my dear wife,
Last night at the third watch I sighed at being apart.
The message you gave with tender thoughts is still with
    me;
I do not know what day I can return home.

27

The silvery red shirt is half covered with dust.[136]
A flickering lamp keeps this body company.
I am like pear blossoms which have already fallen;
Pity the bare branches during the late spring.

28

Xishi[137] always lives in golden houses;
Only the dirt walls and bamboo matted window are left
    for me.
I send a verbal message to the twin swallows between
    the rafters:
Is there a good room looming at the horizon?

29

A drifting duckweed, I arrived a traveller to this
    place.
As I ascend the building, I have painful recollections
    of my native village.
It is because of poverty at home that I am detained here.
It has led to my humiliation, which is truly heartbreaking.

25 上年六月始揚帆：
不料今時到此監。
耗費金錢千數百；
生平孤苦累家兄。

26 舉筆寫詩我卿知：
昨夜三更嘆別離。
情濃囑語今猶在：
未知何日得旋歸。

27 銀紅衫子半蒙塵：
一盞殘燈伴此身。
却似梨花經已落：
可憐零落舊春時。

28 西施盡住黃金屋：
泥壁篷窗獨剩儂。
寄語樑間雙燕子：
天涯可有好房隴。

29 萍飄作客到此方：
登樓感慨思故鄉。
爲着家貧流落此：
致令受辱實心傷。

1 余本作 "留"

156

30

I bemoan the ancient attitude of disparaging military matters and esteeming civil affairs.

It is a pity that I come too late to support the righteous and extirpate the villainous.

Locked up here, I indeed understand that it is because my country is weak.

Sleeping with awls[138] should spur us to develop our country's strength.

31

Random Thoughts While Staying in the Building

For days I have been without freedom on Island.[139]

In reduced circumstances now, I mingle with the prisoners.

Grievances fill my belly; I rely on poetry to express them.

A pile of clods bloat my chest and I wash it with wine.

Because my country is weak, I have become aware of the laws of growth and decay.

In pursuit of wealth, I have come to understand the principles of expansion and diminution.

When I am idle, I have this wild dream

That I have gained the western barbarian's consent to enter America.

32

Bored and filled with a hundred feelings, I am imprisoned in the building.

Seeing the surroundings stirs one who is sad. How can one stop the tears?

I recall the ship starting off for the land of America.

Looking back, the moon has repeated a cycle.

30　輕武重文嗟古風；
　　挽正鋤奸惜來遲。
　　羈此儻知因國弱；
　　眠錐應勵振邦雄。
　　１ 原作 "推"

31　　居樓偶感
　　日處埃窨不自由；
　　蕭然身世混監囚。
　　牢騷滿腹憑詩寫；
　　塊壘撐胸借酒浮。
　　理悟盈虛因國弱；
　　道參消長爲富求。
　　閒來別有疏狂想；
　　得允西奴登美洲。

32　無聊百感困監樓；
　　觸景愁人淚怎收？
　　曾記動輪來美境；
　　迄今回溯月返流。

33

Drifting alone in the ocean, autumn suddenly passed.
I have just gone through ten thousand calamities; still I
am a prisoner from Chu.[140]
When Wu Zixu played his flute, he thought of erasing
his grievances [141]
When Su Ziqing held his tasseled staff, he vowed he
would one day avenge his wrongs.[142]
When Jiyun shot an arrow at the enemy, he was not
doing it to meddle.[143]
Goujian slept on firewood, but he had a reason.[144]
My inflamed liver and bowels are prepared to take life
lightly and engage in a life and death struggle.
Will the blue heavens allow me to fulfill this ambition or
not?

34

We are as one, fellow sufferers with mutual sympathy.[145]
Just like Confucius when he was surrounded at the state
of Chen.[146]
Secretly, I praise your reliance on the strength of
righteousness
To trample the barbarian, rather than letting others do it.

By Xin, using the same rhyme words

35

Traces Left By One From Yingyang[147]

In my lonely drifting life, I experienced great changes.[148]
It is very sad for the innocent to be imprisoned in the
wooden building.
I send words to you gentlemen that you should make
plans to eradicate this grievance.
While you are enjoying yourselves, in particular,
remember our grudge here.

---

33 飄零湖海倏經秋；
萬劫纔過作楚囚。
伍子吹簫懷雪恨；
蘇卿持節誓報仇。
霽雲射矢非多事；
勾踐臥薪却有由。
激烈肝腸輕一決；
蒼天諾否此志酬。

1 余本作 "擊"

34 同病相憐如一身；
恰似仲尼困在陳。
私維君子仗義力；
足戮胡奴弗讓仁。
辛和

35 **滎陽遺蹟**
飄零身世感滄桑；
淒絕無辜困木樓。
寄語諸君謀雪恨；
樂中尤記個中仇。

158

36

Being imprisoned in this wooden shack is precisely the
  cause of my worry.
It is like sitting in jail for committing a crime.
The hundred different abuses are really difficult to
  endure.
My only hope is that my compatriots will avenge this
  grievance.

37

 I especially advise my compatriots not to worry.
We need only remember our confinement in the wooden
  building.
One day after we have united to make our nation strong,
We will then reciprocate in kind to America.

38

A member of the Li[149] household was ready to leave.
In the last month of summer, I arrived in America on
  ship.
After crossing the ocean, the ship docked and I
  waited to go on shore.
Because of the records, the innocent was imprisoned
  in a wooden building.
Reflecting on the event, my heart is vexed and
  depressed.
I composed a poem to rid myself of sadness and
  worry.
At present, my application for admission has not yet
  been dismissed.
As I record the cause of my situation, it really
  provokes my anger.
Sitting here, uselessly delayed for long years and
  months,
I am like a pigeon in a cage.

**Composed as a gift by an overseas Chinese, *illegible*, a
mountain monk from the Town of Iron.**[150]

36 木樓被困正堪憂；
儼然犯罪坐監牢。
百般苛待眞難受；
惟望同胞雪此仇。

37 特勸同胞不可憂；
只須記取困木樓。
他日合羣興邦後；
自將個樣還美洲。

38 李宅人員把身抽；
季夏乘船到美洲。
海過舟灣候上岸；
紀錄無辜困木樓。
念及事情心厭悶；
詩章題首解愁憂。
目下未曾批消案；
錄記情由實可嬲。
在坐虛延長歲月；
此處如籠一隻鳩。

華僑□鐵城山僧題贈
1 原作 "書"

159

39

As a traveller weathering wind and dust, I ran east and
west,
But I never expected now to wind up in a prison.
Because my plan was leaked, I am now in difficult straits
on the mountain.
How will I devise strategy so that the hidden dragon can
emerge?[151]
Wu Xizu, who endured and hid, was able to redress his
grievance.[152]
Sun Bin endured humiliation and was successful in
avenging his wrongs.[153]
I am now being deported back to my country.
Some day when we become rich and strong, we will
annihilate this barbaric nation.

40

For the sake of the mouth, I rushed about and must
tolerate humiliation.
I gritted my teeth, clutched the brush, and recorded the
circumstances.
The day my compatriots become prosperous and return
to China,
They should once more outfit battleships to punish
America.

41

I strongly advise my countrymen not to worry,
Even though you are imprisoned in a wooden building.
Some day after China rises and changes,
She will be adept at using bombs to obliterate America.

42

The commandant at Nanking[154] sent a cable
To urge the people to raise funds to build the nation.
I hope my compatriots will contribute their utmost.
It is enough to avoid perishing.

39　風塵作客走西東：
　　不料今時到監中。
　　因洩機謀山中困：
　　何籌韜略出潛龍¹。
　　子胥忍藏能雪恨：
　　孫臏忍辱復仇功。
　　我今撥回歸國去：
　　他日富強滅番邦。

　　¹ 余本作"籠"

40　爲口奔馳須忍辱：
　　咬牙秉筆錄情由。
　　同胞發達回唐日：
　　再整戰艦伐美洲。

41　特勸同胞不可憂：
　　雖然被困在木樓。
　　他日中華興轉後：
　　擅用炸彈滅美洲。

42　南京留守曾電報：
　　提倡民款建國□。
　　仰望同胞捐盡力：
　　得免淪亡足□□。

43

Japan swallows China.[155]
To unify our efforts, we must think of regulating the
    family.
After regulating the family, the state then becomes
    properly governed.[156]
Upon gaining strength, we will annihilate the dwarves.[157]

44

When a newcomer arrives in America,[158]
He will surely be seized and put in the wooden
    building.
Like a major criminal,
I have already been here one autumn.
The Americans refused me admission;
I have been barred and deported back.
Alongside the ship, the waves are huge.
Returning to the motherland is truly distressing.
We Chinese of a weak nation,
Sigh bitterly at the lack of freedom.
The day our nation becomes strong,
I swear we will cut off the barbarians' heads.

43 日本吞中華；

合力思齊家；

齊家次治國；

富強滅倭奴。

44 新客到美洲；

必遂入木樓。

儼如大犯樣；

在此經一秋。

美國人不准；

批消撥回頭。

船中波浪大；

回國實堪憂。

國弱我華人；

苦嘆不自由。

我國豪強日；

誓斬胡人頭。

1 余本作 "隸"

45

A thousand sorrows and a hatred ten-thousand-fold
burns between my brows.
Hoping to step ashore the American continent is the
most difficult of difficulties.
The barbarians imprison me in this place.
Even a martyr or a hero would change countenance.

46

I clasped hands in parting with my brothers and
classmates.
Because of the mouth,[159] I hastened to cross the American
ocean.
How was I to know that the western barbarians had lost
their hearts and reason?
With a hundred kinds of oppressive laws, they mistreat
us Chinese.[160]
It is still not enough after being interrogated and
investigated several times;
We also have to have our chests examined while naked.
Our countrymen suffer this treatment
All because our country's power cannot yet expand.
If there comes a day when China will be united,
I will surely cut out the heart and bowels of the western
barbarian.

47

Since my imprisonment here, the moon has once again
waxed full.
I still do not know when I will be interrogated.
Family poverty forced me to come and endure hardships.
It is difficult to pour out all the anger and grief in my
heart.
If I could land after only one interrogation,
It would be a slight mitigation of the barbarian's hundred
oppressions.
If I could fulfill my life-long wish,
Even a little suffering would not matter.

45 千愁萬恨燃眉間；
望登美洲難上難。
番奴把我囚困此；
列士英雄亦失顏。

46 握別兄弟與同窗；
爲口奔馳涉美洋。
豈知西奴心理喪；
百般苛例虐我唐。
數次審查猶未了，
還須裸體驗胸膛。
我們同胞遭至此，
皆因國勢未能張。
倘得中華一統日，
定割西奴心與腸。

47 此間囚困月重圓；
審問何時尚未知。
家窮逼我來受苦；
難盡心中憤與悲。
若得一審能上埠；
稍減蠻夷百般欺。
倘能遂我平生願；
雖受苦楚亦唔拘。

48

I bowed farewell to my close friends and went abroad.
How was I to know the barbarians would imprison me?
From antiquity, users of brute force have had no sense of
    justice.
Are there any clever schemes to escape this prison?
If I am deported back to China one day,
Then several months' efforts will have been thrown into
    the water.
What a pity that Feng Tang aged so easily.[161]
Why was it most difficult for Li Guang to win honors?[162]

49

When I began reflecting, I became sad and composed a
    poem.
It was because my family was poor that I left for the
    country of the Flowery Flag.[163]
I only hoped that when I arrived it would be easy to go
    ashore.
Who was to know the barbarians would change the
    regulations?
They stab the ear to test the blood and in addition they
    examine the excrement.[164]
If there is even a shadow of hookworms, one must be
    transferred to undergo a cure.
They took several dozen foreign dollars.[165]
Imprisoned in the hospital, I was miserable with grief
    and sorrow.
I do not know when I will be cured.
If one day I can escape and rise to my aspirations.
I will leave this place for once and for all and not be
    dependent on her,
To avoid humiliation and oppression by the devils.
My fellow villagers seeing this should take heed and
    remember,
I write my wild words to let those after me know.

48

揖別知己出外洋；
豈知胡虜困我身？
自古強權無公理；
有何妙策出牢籠。
一旦撥回歸國去；
數月工程付水中。
可惜馮唐容易老；
何其李廣最難封？

1 余本作 "庚"

49

想起愁來題首詩。
因爲家窮走花旗。
只望來到登岸易；
誰知番奴轉例規？
刺耳驗血兼驗屎；
影有勾蟲須調治。
取得洋蚨數十餘；
困在醫房苦愁悲。
未知何日得痊愈。
若得脱身奮志日，
一排走清唔向倚，
免至凌辱受鬼欺。
梓里一看宜謹記；
寫我狂言留後知。

1 余本作 "派"

50

Abandoning books and inkstone, I drifted across the sea.
The intention was to make a humble person like myself
    famous.
It was difficult to foresee that I would be faced with
    imprisonment on arrival.
Still awaiting fulfillment of my ambition, I will long feel
    aggrieved.
It is enough to cause one to sigh at coming here and
    being lodged like duckweed.
After sacrificing a huge sum of money, I am now being
    disembowelled by the devils.[166]
In this journey I deeply wish to fulfill my ambition.
If not, it will be in vain that my heart breaks in
    confinement.

50 棄書荒硯來飄洋：
意欲把我素心揚。
難料到此遭囹圄：
壯志待酬抱恨長。
堪嘆來此如萍寄：
犧牲巨款受鬼劏[1]。
此行深願酬我志：
否則囚困苦斷腸。

1 余本作"膛"

51

The savage doctors examine for hookworms.
I could not go ashore because fate was not kind.
Why should a young man take his life so lightly?
To whom should I cry out for redress of these terrible
    wrongs?

51 狼醫要驗勾蟲症：
不能登陸運不靈。
青年何苦輕生命：
寃沉二字向誰鳴？

52

Although I had read through four or five loads of poetry
    and history,[167]
I had only one blue shirt[168] when I became old.
The American woman[169] asked what age I was,
Fifty years ago it was 23.

52 讀罷詩書四五担：
老來方得一青衫：
佳人問我年多少：
五十年前二十三。

53

Fifth day of the tenth moon, xinhai year;[170] **Effusion**
  After Moving:
I arrived in the wooden building one week ago.
Whenever someone mentions moving, it distresses me
  excessively.
Gathering all my baggage together, I hurriedly run.
Who would ever know the misery of it all?

54

This unworthy one with the group is grief-stricken.
Who will transmit the news of death back to the village?
I mourn your having ridden the crane to return to the
  dark regions.[171]
A traveller arrived in America on a ship.
Tears enveloped the lonely soul as the cuckoo uttered its
  mournful cry.
Sorrow has led me to dream of travelling to the Terrace
  of Yang.[172]
It is a pity that medicine was wrongly prescribed.
The corpse was nearly cremated to ashes.

53 辛亥十月初五
搬房有感而作

到來木屋一星期；
提起搬屋我極悲。
執齊行李忙忙走；
其中苦楚有誰知？

54 忝屬同羣事感哀。
訃音誰遞故鄉回？
痛君騎鶴歸冥去；
有客乘槎赴美來。
淚鎖孤魂悲杜宇；
愁牽旅夢到陽台。
可憐葯石施醫誤；
險被焚屍一炬灰。

55

The barbarian's cruelty is overwhelming.
Taking advantage of their power, they oppress us Chinese.[173]
All our compatriots meet with such treatment.
It is as if we were criminals locked in a jail cell.

56

Away from home and living in the wooden building, I am secretly grieved.
Splendor fades with the turn of an eye, so be not too earnest.
I leave words with those who will come to Island[174] in the future.
You should raise your head and observe the people.

57

For half a year on Island,[175] we experienced both the bitter and the sweet.
We only part now as I am being deported.
I leave words to my fellow villagers that when they land,
I expect them to always remember the time they spent here.

58

For half a year after I had been refused entry, I heard no news.
Who was to know that today I would be deported back to Tang?[176]
On the ship I will have to endure the waves; tear drops fall.
On a clear night, thinking it over three times, the bitterness is difficult to bear.

59

Again I crossed the ocean to come to America.
I only hope this time I could fulfill my ambition.
Who was to know that Heaven would not will it?
Stubbornly, it refused my entry and caused my imprisonment in the wooden building.

55 番奴狠毒不可當；
倚仗蠻強虐我唐。
大眾同胞遭至此；
猶如罪犯鎖監房。

1 余本作 "狠狠"

56 旅居木屋暗傷神；
轉眼韶光莫認眞。
寄語埃崙將來者；
翹頭應望是中人。

57 埃崙半載同甘苦；
我今撥回始別離，
寄語同鄉上埠日；
務望時記是中期。

58 批消半載無消息；
誰知今日撥回唐？
船中捱浪珠淚落；
清夜三思苦難堪。

59 再歷重洋到美洲；
只望是番把志酬。
豈知天不爲我便；
偏敎批消困木樓。

60

My family was poor, so I was going to Lusong.[177]
Who would have known this would be a prison even for
    those just passing through?
One cannot bear to ask about the loneliness in the
    wooden building.
It is all because of a militarily weak nation with an empty
    national treasury.
I leave word with you gentlemen that you should all
    endeavor together.
Do not forget the national humiliations; arouse
    yourselves to be heroic.

61

I did not expect to be drifting like duckweed to Mexico
    City.[178]
I had been all over the world in three years.
Copper cash did not know me, but that did me no harm.
I was tired of listening to the fusillades of rifles and
    cannonades,[179]
So I risked stealing across the barrier to live in the
    United States.
Who was to know that today I would be punished with
    imprisonment?

62

In January I started to leave for Mexico.
Passage reservations delayed me until mid-autumn.
I had wholeheartedly counted on a quick landing at the
    city,
But the year's almost ending and I am still here in this
    building.

**Last third of the last month of the seventh year of the Republic[180]
Longdu,[181] Xiangshan[182]**

60 家道貧窮走呂宋；
誰知借路亦牢籠？
木樓淒涼不堪問；
皆因兵弱國庫空。
寄語諸君齊發奮；
勿忘國恥振英雄。

61 家徒壁立□□留；
握別妻兒□□舟。
破浪乘風登墨□；
□□□□□□流。
不料浮萍至墨京；
寰球遍地已三年，
青蚨不識無傷我。
悶聽鎗林砲雨聲；
故冒偷關來居美；
誰知今日受囚刑？

62 元月動程赴墨洲；
船位阻延到中秋。
一心指望頻登埠；
年關將及在此樓。

民國七年尾月下浣
香山隆都

167

63

The road is far for the traveller; ten thousand *li*[183] are difficult.
May I advise you not to sneak across the border.
The difficult and dangerous conditions are not worth your inquiries.
These are not idle words.

63 路遠行人萬里難；
　　勸君切勿來偷關。
　　艱險情形堪莫問；
　　斯言不是作爲閒。

64

Wandering footloose here and there, I reminisce about old journeys;
Old acquaintances, living or now dead, each have made his important contribution.
I am, in this life, unfortunately, of Chinese descent;
Enduring humiliation, nursing a grievance; now I am a prisoner of Chu.[184, 185]

64 浪跡江湖憶舊遊；
　　故人生死各千秋。
　　今生不幸爲華裔；
　　忍辱含仇做楚囚。

65

Having not yet crossed the Yellow River, my heart is not at peace;
After crossing the Yellow River, a double stream of tears flow.[186]

65 未過黃河心不息；
　　過了黃河雙淚流。

66

I pray that the day you again enter the cycle of life;
You'll not be a chap with a worthless life from a poor family.[187]

66 祝君再渡巡環日；
　　莫做貧家賤命郎。
　　（據說有一同胞懸探棄世，
　　　翌日即有人寫下以
　　　　上兩句。）

168

FOOTNOTES FOR APPENDIX POEMS

[118] See Note 9.

[119] A festival occurring on the 9th day of the 9th moon.

[120] A precious variety of jade.

[121] See Note 1.

[122] See Note 2.

[123] The Chinese flag from 1912 to 1927 had five horizontal colored stripes: red, yellow, blue, white and black.

[124] Literally, "to lose their gall bladders." According to Chinese traditional beliefs, courage resides in the gall bladder.

[125] This poem was included by Smiley Jann in his collection, but it was not originally on the wall.

[126] Admission into the United States.

[127] See Note 14.

[128] Better known as Chang'e, goddess living in the moon.

[129] Village in Zhongshan District.

[130] See Note 108.

[131] See Note 2.

[132] Tong Guan is a strategic pass in Shenxi. The rugged terrain there makes it easy to defend against attackers.

[133] See Note 49.

[134] See Note 2.

[135] The mail service.

[136] "Covered with dust" is a term used to describe fleeing in troubled times.

[137] A famous beauty of the State of Yue during the Spring and Autumn period. She was sent by King Goujian of Yue as a gift to King Fucha (495 -477 B.C.) of Wu to divert him from concentrating on state affairs so that the Yue state could mobilize her forces to attack Wu and avenge a previous humiliating defeat. Xishi is used here as an oblique reference to Westerners or Americans, since "Xi" is the character for "West" and Xishi is a beauty or "meiren," also the term for "American."

[138] See Note 4 on Su Qin.

[139] See Note 2.

[140] See Note 99.

[141] See Note 18.

[142] See Note 30.

[143] Nan Jiyun (? - 757 A.D.). During the An Lushan rebellion (755 - 760 A.D.), the rebel army surrounded Suiyang (in the present Henan Province). Nan was one of the defenders of the besieged city and shot the enemy general in the left eye with one arrow.

[144] See Note 78.

[145] This poem uses the same rhyme words as poem 46 in the main text.

[146] See Note 27.

[147] Yingyang, a district in Henan Province, is attributed to be the place of origin of the Zheng (usually Jang or Jung in the United States) clan.

[148] See Note 23.

[149] More commonly "Lee" in the U.S.

[150] i.e., Shiqi. See Note 42.

[151] From the Yi Jing. This is symbolic of a sage who is concealed and not in prominence.

[152] See Note 18.

[153] Sun Bin and Pang Juan (? - 314 B.C.) studied together during the Warring States Period (475 - 221 B.C.). After completion, Pang served as an official in the state of Wei (in the present Shanxi province). When Sun came to seek a position, Pang became apprehensive that Sun would prove to be more capable. He then falsely accused Sun of conspiring with the neighboring state of Qi (in the present Shandong province). As a result, Sun was punished by cutting off his kneecaps so that he could no longer walk. Subsequently, Sun served the state of Qi and in 341 B.C. led a Qi army to attack Wei. Pang was defeated and slain in the campaign. Sun Bin is known today for a book of military tactics attributed to him.

[154] Briefly the capital of the Provisional Government of the Republic of China after the 1911 Revolution. Also the capital of the Nationalist Government from 1927 to 1949.

[155] The original of this poem had seven characters per line; however, the first two characters in each line were illegible.

[156] This comes from "The Great Learning," a chapter of Book of Rites, incorporated as one of the Confucian "Four Books." The text is as follows: ". . . Things being investigated, knowledge become complete. Then knowledge being complete, their thoughts were sincere. Their thoughts being sincere, their hearts were then rectified. Their hearts being rectified, their persons were cultivated. Their persons being cultivated, their families were regulated. Their families being regulated, their states were rightly governed. Their states being rightly governed, the entire Kingdom was made tranquil and happy. . ."

[157] A derogatory term for the Japanese.

[158] This poem is the same as Poem 63 in the main text except that it has two additional lines. Also, each line has five characters instead of the four characters found in Poem 63.

[159] i.e., to feed oneself, to make a living.

[160] Literally, "men of Tang." This is the colloquial Cantonese term for the Chinese.

[161] Feng Tang was a capable official serving Emperor Wen (179 - 157 B.C.) of the Han dynasty. Later, when Emperor Wu (149 - 87 B.C.) was seeking men of talent, Feng's name was recommended. But by that time, he was more than 90 years old. His son was appointed in his stead.

[162] Li Guang (? - 119 B.C.) was a general serving Emperor Wu of the Han dynasty. He was renowned for his many victories over the Xiongnu nomads. However, he was never conferred a noble title. Li Ling (See Note 85) was his grandson.

[163] See Note 9.

[164] Examination for filiariasis and uncinariasis.

[165] Probably payment for medical treatment.

[166] A colloquial term for non-Chinese, particularly those not of the Mongolian race.

[167] Two of the Confucian classics: Shi Jing (Classic of Poetry) and Shu Jing (Classic of History). In ancient times, books were written on bamboo slivers; hence, each "book" was very bulky.

[168] This is derived from "qingyi" or "blue clothing." The lower social classes in China customarily wore blue colored clothing.

[169] The original characters "jiaren" literally mean, "The beautiful woman," a synonym for "meiren," which is a homonym for "American."

[170] i.e., 1911.

[171] i.e., death. In Chinese mythology, cranes are connected with immortals.

[172] King Huai of Chu (328 - 299 B.C.) met a female immortal in a dream and had sexual relations with her. She was found every morning and evening at the foot of the Terrace of Yang, which has come to be used as an allusion to a place where men and women meet for sexual liaisons.

[173] See Note 160.

[174] See Note 2.

[175] See Note 2.

[176] The text uses Tang for Mountains of Tang. See note 37.

[177] Mexico. See Note 83.

[178] The preceding four lines are largely illegible. The contents appear to state that his family was poor and that he had to leave his wife and child to go to Mexico.

[179] Probably refers to battles in Mexican civil wars.

[180] 1918.

[181] An area in Zhongshan district, from which many immigrants originated.

[182] See Note 6.

[183] See Note 1.

[184] See note 99.

[185] The person who provided this poem was detained during the early 1920's.

[186] The person who provided this couplet was detained during the early 1920's.

[187] This is said to be a commentary written on the wall the day after a detainee had hung himself. The person who provided this couplet was detained during the early 1920's.

SOURCES OF POEMS

Due to the fact that many poems on the walls were barely legible, as well as the fact that various transcribers had apparently made editorial changes, a number of works exist in several versions. The editors have chosen for this collection the versions they believe to be closest to the original, regardless of their artistic merits as compared with the other variations. The sources are as follows:
Currently on the barrack walls—

Takahashi's photographs: Main Text Nos. 3, 4, 6, 11, 13, 14, 20, 21, 23-25, 31, 36, 37, 45, 49, 51-53, 62-65, 67, 68; Appendix Nos. 2, 3, 7, 16, 30, 35, 38, 42, 43, 53, 60-63.

Kearny Street Workshop rubbings: Main Text Nos. 43, 44, 57.

San Francisco Weekly: Main Text Nos. 2, 8, 9, 34, 46; Appendix Nos. 1, 11, 15, 31, 34, 35.

Three Generations of Chinese: Main Text Nos. 69.

Copied by Tet Yee, 1932: Main Text Nos. 1, 5, 7, 15-17, 19, 22, 26, 28, 29, 32, 33, 35, 38-42, 47, 48, 50, 54, 55, 58, 59, 61, 66; Appendix Nos. 12, 13, 17, 19-22, 24, 25, 29, 32, 33, 36, 39, 40, 41, 44-46, 48-51, 54, 55, 58, 59.

Copied by Smiley Jann, 1971: Main Text Nos. 10, 18, 60; Appendix Nos. 5, 6, 8, 10, 18, 37, 47, 56, 57.

Chinese Pacific Weekly: Main Text Nos. 10, 27; Appendix Nos. 64-66.

Allen T. Fong: Appendix No. 14.

Tien Sheng Weekly: Main Text No. 30; Appendix Nos. 4, 26-28, 52.

Yuehai Chunqiu, 1923 (Set of five poems, of which two, with slight textual differences, are now on the walls [Main Text No. 62; Appendix No. 16]. The possibility exists that the wall poems may have been merely quotes from this work.) Main Text No. 56; Appendix Nos. 9, 23.

SOURCES OF PHOTOGRAPHS

Page
Cover Angel Island and Alcatraz, Ruby Star
   9 A door into imprisonment, Chris Huie
  11 Male detainees on hospital steps, National Archives
  13 Immigrants' first view of Angel Island barracks, National Park Service
  15 Women's infirmary, National Archives
  17 Tye Leung with Deaconess Katharine Maurer, Frederick Schulze
  18 Chinese kitchen help, National Archives
  21 A page from a coaching book, Chris Huie
  24 Exercise yard, Frances Maurer Schneider
  26 (Above) Dining hall, National Park Service
     (Below) Mealtime, California Historical Society
  27 Burning administration building, National Park Service
  28 Dormitory, Paul Chow
  29 Boat at pier, National Park Service
  30 En route to *Gam Saan*, San Francisco Maritime Museum

32-33 Immigrants aboard ship, National Archives
50-51 Interrogation scene, National Archives
82-83 Women detainees with missionary, California Historical Society
98-99 Physical examination, National Archives
120-121 Empty bunks, National Archives
135 Carving from barrack wall, Mak Takahashi
147 Boy on Angel Island, Philip Choy
148-149 Contemporary photo of men's dormitory, Leland Wong

ENGLISH BIBLIOGRAPHY

Angel Island Immigration Station Historical Advisory Committee. *Report and Recommendations on Angel Island Immigration Station.* San Francisco: 1976

Bamford, Mary. *Angel Island; the Ellis Island of the West.* Chicago: Woman's American Baptist Home Mission Society, 1917.

Chow, Christopher & Yu, Connie Young. "Angel Island and Chinese Immigration." *San Francisco Journal.* June 30, July 21, August 4, 11, 18, 25, 1976; revised version, published April 25, 1979.

Fu, Chi Hao. "My Reception in America." *Outlook.* August 10, 1907, pp. 770-773.

Lai, H.M. "Angel Island Immigration Station." *Bridge Magazine.* April, 1977, pp. 4-8.

Lai, H.M. "The Chinese Experience at Angel Island." *East West Chinese American Journal.* February 11, 18, 25, 1976.

Lai, H.M. "Island of the Immortals: Angel Island Immigration Station and the Chinese Immigrants." *California History.* Spring, 1978, pp. 88-103.

Lim, Genny & Yung, Judy. "Our Parents Never Told Us." *California Living, San Francisco Examiner & Chronicle.* January 23, 1977, pp. 6-9.

McDonald, Marshall & Associates. *Report and Recommendations on Angel Island. 1769-1966.* Oakland: 1966.

Power, Keith. "The Ellis Island of the West." *San Francisco Chronicle.* November 25, 1974, p. 5.

Sun, Shirley. *Three Generations of Chinese—East and West.* Oakland Museum: 1973, pp. 27-29, 33.

U.S. Dept. of Commerce and Labor. Bureau of Immigration and Naturalization. *Annual Report of the Commissioner General of Immigration for the Fiscal Year . . . 1910-1913.*

U.S. Dept. of Labor. *Annual Report of the Secretary of Labor, For the Fiscal Year . . . 1928-1947.*

U.S. Dept. of Labor. Bureau of Immigration. *Annual Report of the Commissioner General of Immigration, for the Fiscal Year . . . 1914-1933.*

Wang, Ling-chi. "The Yee Version of Poems from the Chinese Immigration Station." *Asian American Review.* Berkeley: University of California, 1976, pp. 117-126.

Yu, Connie Young. "Rediscovered Voices: Chinese Immigrants and Angel Island." *Amerasia Journal.* Vol. 4, No. 2, 1977, pp. 123-139.

Yu, Yao Pei. "The Treatment of the Chinese by the United States Immigration Service." *Chinese Student.* August, 1936.

Yung, Judy. "A Bowlful of Tears: Chinese Women Immigrants on Angel Island." *Frontiers.* Volume 2, No. 2, 1977, pp. 52-55.

參攷資料

黃遵憲: "逐客篇"(人境廬詩草箋註, 第126至130
　　　頁, 九龍: 中華書局, 1963年刊)

阿英編: 反美華工禁約文學集(上海: 中華書局,
　　　1960年刊)

———: "木屋拘留序"(三藩市: 世界日報, 1910
　　　年1月16日)

———: "華僑血淚"(又名"關博士力爭苛例")(三藩
　　　市: 少年中國晨報, 1911年2月至4月,
　　　不全)

———: "木屋拘囚吃盡苦"(金山歌集, 第13B至
　　　14A頁, 三藩市: 大光書林, 1911年刊)

———: "埃崙僑胞致各界書"
　　　(三藩市: 世界日報, 1923年8月24日)

———: "美洲被囚困木屋疏"(粵海春秋, 第23B
　　　至26A頁, 廣州, 1923年刊)

———: "天使島客被困"; "天涯窘苦中之哀思";
　　　"對美新移民律之悲憤"(粵曲精華, 第1至
　　　7頁, 三藩市: 金門樂群社, 1925年刊)
　　　又見粵調歌曲菁華, 第103至108頁, 三藩
　　　市: 新大陸圖書館, 1926年刊)

王德恩: "留美移民局被拘記"(奉天省: 東三省留美
　　　學生年報, 第一號, 第200至240頁,
　　　1926年8月15日刊)

亞　程: "羈留丁治埃崙有感"(三藩市: 公論晨報,
　　　1931年1月2日)

鄭文舫: "金山客的自述"(上海: 人間世, 第15至
　　　16頁, 1935年3月15日)

鄭文舫：“秋蓬集，集弱者心聲卷”(手抄本，１９３２年，
　　　　４０頁)

余耀培：“美國移民局拘禁入境華僑慘狀”(芝加哥：
　　　　留美學生月刊，第一卷，第５號，第15至
　　　　18頁，1936年４月)

追　陳：“天使島”(三藩市：時代報，1973年11月
　　　　14日)

──：“埃崙詩選”(三藩市：舊金山週報，1974
　　　　年４月10日)

景　南：“藍烟通與總統輪”(三藩市：太平洋週報，
　　　　1974年11月14日)

景　南：“天使島”(同上，１９７４年11月21日)

景　南：“天使島上的帶信人”(同上，１９７４年11
　　　　月28日)

景　南：“天使島的審問”(同上，１９７４年12月5日)

張正平：“天使島的老監囚”(三藩市：東西報，
　　　　1976年12月15日)

張正平：“華人移民的血淚史詩，天使島之歌”(同
　　　　上，1977年２月2，9，16，23日)

方大明：“‘木樓’寫眞”(三藩市：太平洋週報，
　　　　1978年８月24日)

方民希：“木樓題壁詩註釋”(同上，1978年８月
　　　　24日)

盤古皇：“詩十二首”(三藩市：天聲週報，1979年
　　　　７月17日)